MONARCHIES

EXPLORING WORLD GOVERNMENTS

ABDO
Publishing Company

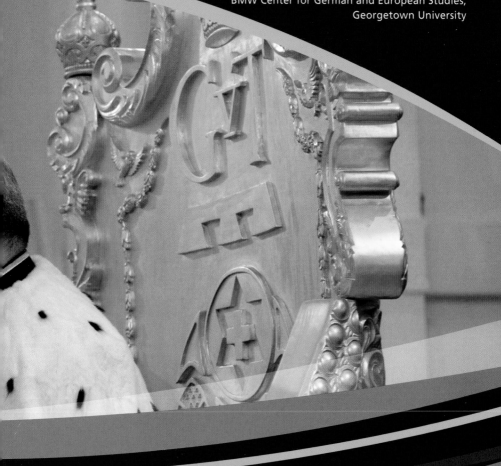

MONARCHIES

by Diane Marczely Gimpel

Content Consultant
Jeffrey J. Anderson, Professor and Director
BMW Center for German and European Studies,
Georgetown University

CREDITS

Published by ABDO Publishing Company, 8000 West 78th Street, Edina, Minnesota 55439. Copyright © 2011 by Abdo Consulting Group, Inc. International copyrights reserved in all countries. No part of this book may be reproduced in any form without written permission from the publisher. The Essential Library™ is a trademark and logo of ABDO Publishing Company.

Printed in the United States of America, North Mankato, Minnesota
112010
012011

Editor: Erika Wittekind
Copy Editor: Jennifer Anderson
Interior Design and Production: Becky Daum
Cover Design: Becky Daum

Photo Credits: New Zealand Herald/AP Images, cover, 2, 3; Ian Poole/iStockphoto, 9; Bain News Service/Library of Congress, 10; Arthur Edwards/AP Images, 17; POLFOTO, Tariq Mikkel Khan/AP Images, 21; Ray Roper/iStockphoto, 23; MAP/AP Images, 28; Matson Photo Service/Library of Congress, 33; Paolo Gaetano Rocco/iStockphoto, 35; Duncan Walker/iStockphoto, 40; Library of Congress, 45, 62; Lea Brothers & Company/Library of Congress, 49; Gurinder Osan/AP Images, 55; Georgios Kollidas/iStockphoto, 60; Owen Humphreys /PA Wire/AP Images, 69; Kyodo via AP Images, 77; Saurabh Das/AP Images, 81; Gina Sanders/Fotolia, 91; Ron Edmonds/AP Images, 103; AP Images, 113, 133; Michael Dunlea, Pool/AP Images, 116; Bertil Erickson, Scanpix/AP Images, 123; iStockphoto, 137

Library of Congress Cataloging-in-Publication Data
Gimpel, Diane, 1963-
  Monarchies / by Diane Gimpel.
     p. cm. -- (Exploring world governments)
  Includes bibliographical references.
  ISBN 978-1-61714-792-0
  1. Monarchy. 2. Kings and rulers. 3. Queens. I. Title.
  JC375.G56 2011
  321.8'7--dc22
                                    2010045194

Table of Contents

What Is Government?

In the earliest, simplest societies, government as we know it did not exist. Family or tribal elders made decisions, and their powers were limited. As civilizations grew, governments developed to organize societies and to protect them from outside threats. As societies have grown in complexity, so have the governments that organize them. In this way, organizing society has led to massive bureaucracies with many offices and roles.

As of 2010, there were more than 190 countries, each with its own government. Two governments may look very similar on paper even though political life inside those countries varies greatly. Every government is different because it is influenced by its country's history, culture, economics, geography, and even psychology.

Still, governments share some main roles. Today, a main function of governments is to protect citizens from outside threats. This has evolved into the vast arena of international relations, including military alliances and trade agreements. Governments also organize power in a society. However, how power is acquired—through elections, heredity, or force—varies, as does who exercises it—one person, a few, or many.

Ideally, governments balance the rights of individuals against the needs of the whole society. But who defines those needs? Is it leaders chosen by universal suffrage, or is it a single dictator who assumed power through force? How are individual rights protected? The answers to these questions distinguish one form of government from another.

Another role of government is preserving internal order—that is, order as defined by those in power. While keeping order might mean prosecuting violent criminals in a democracy, in a dictatorship, it could mean prosecuting dissenters. Governments also look out for the welfare of their citizens. All modern governments provide some form of social services, ranging from education to housing to health care.

Governments are often involved in their national economies. Involvement can run the full spectrum—from completely planning the economy to merely levying taxes and allowing a free market to operate. Governments also regulate the private lives of citizens—from issuing marriage licenses in a democracy to enforcing specific styles of dress in a theocracy.

While all governments have some characteristics in common, the world's governments take many forms and make decisions differently. How does a government decide what individual rights to give its citizens? How are laws enforced? What happens when laws are broken? The answers to such questions depend on the political system at hand. ⌘

1

Queen Elizabeth II, a Modern Monarch

When King George VI died in 1952, his eldest daughter, Elizabeth, succeeded him on the British throne. No one contested the transition of power to Elizabeth II. However, there was a problem. Elizabeth, of the House of Windsor, was married to Prince Philip of the House of Mountbatten. Because English law held that children of a marriage took their father's name, it appeared the name of the royal house was about to change from Windsor to Mountbatten. Some members of Elizabeth's family, as well as officials

Windsor Castle

Winston Churchill

in the nation's government, strongly opposed such a change.

One problem was political. Prime Minister Winston Churchill was at political odds with Lord Louis Mountbatten, head of the House of Mountbatten and Philip's uncle. Another issue was that the Windsor name was popular with the public. The family had, in fact, carefully chosen this name to suit the taste of the British people. Before 1917, the British royal family had been known as the House of Saxe-Coburg-Gothe. But as the country battled Germany in

World War I, the family's German roots caused public discomfort. In response, they adopted the English surname of Windsor. Robert Lacey, a biographer of Queen Elizabeth II, explained the motivation for the 1917 name change this way: "A new dynasty had been created to meet public demand. . . . The reason was obvious, and would become the bottom line and guiding principle of the new House of Windsor. It was what the people wanted."[1]

To Churchill in 1952, what was important to the people mattered more than English law or tradition. Philip's personal wish, on the other hand, was that his children be named after him. In the end, the queen did what Churchill believed the people would want: she used her name, and not her husband's.

In the years following, the pressure of public opinion would influence many more of the queen's decisions. For example, her coronation ceremony was to have been a private event. However, after a public outcry, it was broadcast live on television. In 1997, when her former daughter-in-law, Princess Diana of Wales, died in a car crash, the queen was criticized for not showing grief. The queen bowed to public pressure again. She flew a flag at half-mast over Buckingham Palace on the day of the funeral and delivered an internationally televised address.

Power of the People

The compromises made by Queen Elizabeth are common among monarchs today, who find they must bend to the will of the government and of the people. Although the term *monarchy* may conjure images of all-powerful rulers, most modern monarchs do not have absolute power. All but a handful of the world's 44 monarchies today are constitutional monarchies, in which the monarch's actions are governed by laws that greatly limit their authority.

BRITISH PARLIAMENT

The nations that call Queen Elizabeth II their head of state all operate under a parliamentary system of government. In the United Kingdom, the British Parliament is a bicameral legislature, meaning it is comprised of two main bodies. One chamber, called the House of Lords, has members who have been appointed, as opposed to elected. They include high-ranking judges, high-ranking clergy from the Church of England, and accomplished citizens who hold titles given by the monarch or who have been chosen by fellow members of the titled nobility.

The stronger of the British Parliament's two chambers is the House of Commons. The people elect members of the House of Commons. The leader of the majority party typically becomes the prime minister, or head of government. He or she then chooses the cabinet, also from the ruling party. This group introduces legislation and runs the government departments. Most of the cabinet members come from the House of Commons, although the speaker of the House of Lords, called the lord chancellor, also holds a cabinet seat.

Power in a constitutional monarchy comes from the people, not from the monarch. The people elect representatives to make laws and other governmental decisions on their behalf. Kings, queens, princes, dukes, and emperors have ceremonial roles and act as national symbols. They cannot make laws.

It was not always so. The English monarchy ruled with virtually unchecked power until 1215. That year, under threat of revolt, King John signed the Magna Carta, a groundbreaking document that protected subjects' rights and established that the monarch could not operate above the law. Soon after, a group of noblemen created the British Parliament, its legislature. By the eighteenth century, Parliament had more power in the government than the sovereign did.

Elizabeth II Learns to Be Queen

Before becoming queen, Elizabeth II was educated about government and the monarchy. At age 13, she began studying constitutional history under the tutelage of Sir Henry Marten, an administrator of Eton College, a private school for boys. One of her textbooks was *Anson's Law and Custom of the Constitution,* which taught her in no uncertain terms that the British sovereign was no longer in charge. As biographer Robert Lacey wrote, "The message of Anson and Marten was clear: Parliament was king. The era when monarchs called or dissolved Parliaments without the advice of elected ministers was dismissed as 'the days before responsible government.'"[2]

When Elizabeth turned 21, she gave a radio address that made it clear she was dedicated to working for her subjects. Elizabeth said: "I declare before you all that my whole life whether it be long or short shall be devoted to your service and the service of our great imperial family to which we all belong."[3] Four years later, in 1952, her father King George VI died, and Elizabeth became queen.

The Queen of England's Limited Role

The monarch of England, who as of 2010 was Queen Elizabeth II, cannot make war without the consent of Parliament, nor can she make law. Parliament makes the laws, and the monarch is required to approve them. The British constitution also requires monarchs to act as consultants to political leaders. The queen does that by meeting once a week with the United Kingdom's prime minister, who is the nation's head of the government. The queen has several other ceremonial duties. She is required to open each new session of Parliament, at which time she reads a speech written by the majority party that describes its legislative agenda. She also dissolves Parliament at the end of each session, when Parliament stops working and new elections are held.

It is the queen's responsibility to appoint the prime minister of the Parliament. The appointment traditionally goes to the leader of the party that, by election, wins the majority of seats in

Parliament's House of Commons—the dominant of Parliament's two chambers. The queen herself is not associated with any political party and takes no sides politically. In fact, the queen is not allowed to vote, to preserve the appearance of her political neutrality. "She's above politics," says Ingrid Seward, editor of *Majesty* magazine. "Her subjects know that she has their well-being at heart."[4]

The queen's constitutional role goes beyond Parliament. In the nation's judiciary, the queen appoints senior judges and also can grant pardons. But those tasks are done on the advice of elected officials, which she must follow. As head of the Church of England, the queen appoints

COMMONWEALTH REALMS

The Commonwealth realms are 16 countries that recognize Queen Elizabeth II as their monarch, although each has an otherwise independent government. They include the United Kingdom, Antigua and Barbuda, Australia, New Zealand, Barbados, Canada, Jamaica, Belize, Papua New Guinea, Saint Kitts and Nevis, Saint Vincent and the Grenadines, Tuvalu, Grenada, Solomon Islands, Saint Lucia, and the Bahamas. The Commonwealth realms are among the 54 members of the Commonwealth of Nations, a voluntary association of nations that is headed by the queen and that work together in the common interests of their citizens. Most Commonwealth nations, including India and South Africa, once were under British rule.

the church's archbishops and bishops, but chooses from nominees selected by a church commission. The queen also makes appearances on behalf of charities and performs ceremonial functions, including handing out official awards to citizens. Among such awards is knighthood, bestowed upon men who have shown distinction in arts, science, law, business, education, and public service. One of those knighted by the queen was Paul McCartney, a former member of the Beatles.

The monarch of England also takes on the role of ambassador to the rest of the world. Elizabeth II frequently meets with dignitaries of other nations, both when they visit England and when she visits those countries. Elizabeth II is queen of 16 other countries, known as the Commonwealth realms. The Commonwealth realms all share the queen as their monarch, although each has its own independent government. The queen is also head of the Commonwealth of Nations, an intergovernmental association

PRINCE PHILIP

In 1969, Prince Philip, husband of the United Kingdom's Queen Elizabeth II, explained the role of the modern monarchy:

It is a complete misconception to imagine the monarchy exists in the interest of the monarch. It doesn't. It exists in the interest of the people. If at any time any nation feels that the system is unacceptable, then it is up to them to change it.[5]

Queen Elizabeth II reads her speech to the House of Lords during the State Opening of Parliament in 2010.

of Commonwealth realms and former British colonies.

A Symbol and Celebrity

Performing her duties, Elizabeth II has become a focus for national identity as well as for unity among the diverse populations of the United Kingdom and the Commonwealth realms. An editorial published in 2002 in the *Ottawa Citizen* newspaper explained:

> *The Queen is engaged in symbolic expressions not only of the monarchy's presence within a nation, but of the nation's own self-understanding. To the degree these symbolic acts have meaning to people, the monarchy creates a sort of civic authenticity.*[6]

18

For some, the queen also serves as a personification of the nation. Explains David Culver, a retired Royal Air Force officer: "As a member of the armed forces, I swore my allegiance to the queen. Yes, it's the politicians in government that decide on going to war. But, ultimately, the loyalty is to the queen."[7] Monarchs elsewhere in the world serve the same function—as a face that helps define the concept of a nation.

> "The Crown is a mirror of our best selves. When the Governor General, as the representative of the Queen, awards medals of bravery, she is saying to the recipients that the head of the Canadian state acknowledges on behalf of all Canadians that person's worth and contribution to society."[8]
>
> —David Smith, political scientist, University of Saskatchewan

Monarchs such as Elizabeth II nowadays find themselves not only the focus of national identity but also the focus of curiosity. They and their family members have become celebrities—people who are celebrated simply for being well known. Their romances, their fashion choices, and their personal lives are publicized in the press and analyzed by the public. In the 1940s, Elizabeth II's romance with Prince Philip drew unwanted attention. Her sister Margaret's involvement with a divorced man became news in 1952, around the same time as Elizabeth's coronation. Later, the dissolution of Princess Margaret's marriage to Antony Armstrong-Jones became a public matter.

The romances of Elizabeth's children attracted even more attention, especially those of her eldest son and heir to the throne, Prince Charles. In particular, the public spotlight focused on Charles's courtship of, marriage to, and subsequent divorce of Lady Diana Spencer. As an attractive young woman involved in many charities, Diana became a darling of the British public and was often hounded by the press. Her death in a car accident in 1997 was blamed in part on press photographers, who were chasing her car in an attempt to get photographs of her with a new boyfriend. Diana and Charles's sons, William and Harry, have also been the subject of public interest now that they are grown and have romances of their own. In this experience, Elizabeth II and her family are not alone among the world's royalty. It is one more example of how the desire of the people is king in the life of a monarch. ⌘

2

What Is a Monarchy?

When citizens of the United Kingdom sing their national anthem, they ask God to save the queen and to "send her victorious, happy and glorious, long to reign over us."[1] The nation's currency has the image of their queen upon it. Members of the armed forces swear their allegiance to the queen. This has been the case since 1952, when Queen Elizabeth II inherited the role of sovereign. When she dies, her eldest son, Charles, will take over. Then, the anthem will change to "God Save the King." His image

Danish Queen Margrethe walks through the streets of Elsingore, Denmark, on October 20, 2010.

will show on currency, and the armed forces will swear allegiance to him.

All of this happens because the people of the United Kingdom live in a monarchy: a governmental system in which ceremonial or actual power is held by one person, usually for life and usually because of heredity. Monarchs may be kings, queens, princes, dukes, emirs, sultans, and emperors. Even the Roman Catholic pope has been considered a monarch. As of 2010, 44 nations had monarchies. These include the 16 Commonwealth realms headed by Queen Elizabeth II.

THE WORLD'S MONARCHIES

The world's monarchies include Andorra, Antigua and Barbuda, Australia, the Bahamas, Bahrain, Barbados, Belgium, Belize, Bhutan, Brunei, Cambodia, Canada, Denmark, Grenada, Holy See (Vatican City), Jamaica, Japan, Jordan, Kuwait, Lesotho, Liechtenstein, Luxembourg, Malaysia, Monaco, Morocco, Netherlands, New Zealand, Norway, Oman, Papua New Guinea, Qatar, Saint Kitts and Nevis, Saint Lucia, Saint Vincent and the Grenadines, Saudi Arabia, Solomon Islands, Spain, Swaziland, Sweden, Thailand, Tonga, Tuvalu, United Arab Emirates, and the United Kingdom.

Nominal Monarchies

Of the nations that have monarchy governments, the vast majority have a nominal monarch. A nominal monarch is one who holds power in name only; that is, the person's title stands for the power of the nation, but he or she operates as a figurehead or a national symbol. A nominal monarch may preside over national ceremonies, visit other countries as a national representative, and meet with visiting foreign dignitaries. A nominal monarch does not hold much, if any, governmental authority.

Nominal monarchs typically exist in constitutional monarchies, the most common type. In a constitutional monarchy, the monarch's power is limited by a constitution, or a rule of law. Usually, but not always, the constitution is a written document. In the United Kingdom, for example, no written constitution exists. The constitution is comprised of statutes as well as customs and conventions. However, the United Kingdom does have a written Bill of Rights, which was adopted in 1689. Among other things, the Bill of Rights states that the power to execute and suspend laws, to have a standing army in peacetime, and to raise money rests with Parliament, not with the king or queen. Previously, monarchs had asserted their right to perform those duties. Most countries with constitutional monarchies have parliamentary democracies, in which the people elect politicians to make the laws and to run the government.

Rules for Rulers

One example of a constitutional monarchy is Sweden, where King Carl XVI Gustaf was the monarch in 2010. The nation's Constitution Act, enacted in 1974, dictates that the king cannot act alone. The act defines the king's role as head of state, performing ceremonial and representative duties and acting as a national symbol. He serves as the foremost representative of the military, opens the Riksdag—Sweden's parliament—each year, makes state visits to other countries, hosts foreign heads of state who visit Sweden, and chairs the nation's Advisory Council on Foreign Affairs. He also heads the special cabinet council that convenes when the government changes. Other than that, according to the Constitution Act, "all public power in Sweden derives from the people."[2] The people elect representatives to the Riksdag every four years. The Riksdag exercises the government's power by making and executing laws.

Monarchies are usually characterized by hereditary rule. Hereditary rule means the position is passed from generation to

CONSTITUTION

A constitution is a set of rules for government. It defines the responsibilities of a government's officials and institutions. It can be one written document, as is the case with the Constitution of the United States of America, or a collection of written documents and customs, as is the case with the United Kingdom.

Ideally, a constitution protects the rights of citizens and allows them to have a say in the government. Woodrow Wilson, the twenty-eighth president of the United States, wrote in his 1908 work, *Constitutional Government in the United States:* "A constitutional government is one whose powers have been adapted to the interests of its people and to the maintenance of individual liberty."[3]

A stamp displays the image of Swedish King Carl XVI Gustaf.

generation within a family and is a lifetime role. In Sweden, King Carl XVI Gustaf is a member of a dynasty that began in 1818 with the king's ancestor Jean Bernadotte. Bernadotte was a French military officer who had contacts among Swedish soldiers. When Sweden needed a new monarch because the old dynasty was dying out, its parliament elected Bernadotte to the throne. The move kept alive a dynastic monarchy government that dates back more than 1,000 years. In Japan, the world's oldest hereditary monarchy, the emperorship, has been passed along for perhaps as long as 2,600 years.

Exceptions to the hereditary rule exist, however. In Cambodia, Malaysia, and the United Arab Emirates, the monarchs are of royal descent, but a selection process determines who will take the throne. In the European country of Andorra, heredity plays no role. One of Andorra's two princes is the president of France, and the other is the bishop of Seu d'Urgell in Spain. In Vatican City, the ruler is the Roman Catholic pope, who is elected by certain members of the Roman Catholic Church's clergy. The pope rules not only Vatican City—a tiny sovereign state with only 800 residents—but also the Holy See, the central government of the Roman Catholic Church. The Roman Catholic Church has more than 1 billion members worldwide.

CORRUPTION

Corruption is sometimes a concern in governments that allow rulers unchecked power. A famous quote by British historian and moralist Lord Acton expresses this idea: "Power tends to corrupt, and absolute power corrupts absolutely."[5]

Absolute Monarchies

While the pope is an example of an elected monarch, he also can be considered an example of an absolute monarch. The Fundamental Law of Vatican City State, decreed by the late Pope John Paul II in 2000, says: "The Supreme Pontiff, Sovereign of Vatican City state, has the fullness of legislative, executive and judicial powers."[4] An absolute monarch is an autocrat who has authority over the state—a sovereign territory—and authority over the government—the organization that makes and enforces laws in a sovereign land.

In most absolute monarchies, the constitution, or body of laws, may have been written by the monarch, who is the only one authorized to change it. However, in some cases, the constitution may place limits on what the monarch can do. Additionally, absolute monarchs may be constrained or influenced by religious leaders, other members of their dynasty, a class of wealthy or noble citizens, or by the military.

Absolute monarchies are sometimes referred to as traditional monarchies because absolute rule was a common characteristic of monarchies when the form of government came into existence many centuries ago. Some governments that are still considered to be absolute monarchies include Vatican City in Europe; Swaziland in Africa; and Brunei, Oman, Qatar, and Saudi Arabia in the Middle East. In none of those countries can the inhabitants choose their national leaders.

Saudi Arabia: An Absolute Monarchy

Perhaps the strongest and most widely known absolute monarchy is the Kingdom of Saudi Arabia, the third Arabian state ruled by the Saud family dynasty since the eighteenth century. The kingdom of Saudi Arabia was founded in 1932 by King Abdul Aziz Al Saud, a Saud family

Morocco's King Mohammed VI delivers a speech during the opening session in the Morocco Parliament on October 8, 2010.

member who began consolidating his power in the Arabian Peninsula in 1902 with his conquest of Riyadh, now Saudi Arabia's capital city. The five kings who have ruled following King Abdul's death have all been sons of the founding king, including King Abdullah, who is monarch as of 2010.

The Basic Law of Government decreed by King Abdullah's predecessor, King Fahd, pro-scribes how the Saudi government operates. The Basic Law declares the government a monarchy, with the right to rule confined to the sons and grandsons of the founding king. The king sets and implements government policy with the help of ministers he appoints. He is commander in chief of the nation's armed forces, for which he appoints officers, and he has the power to mobilize the armed forces and declare war.

The king also appoints judges. The United States Department of State, in its 2009 Human Rights Report, observed that the Saudi king had power over the judiciary. The report states: "In practice, the judiciary was not independent, as it was required to cooperate with the executive and legislative authorities, with the king as arbiter."[6] The Basic Law further declares the Holy Koran, which is Islam's holy book of scripture, and the traditions of Islam's founder, the Prophet Muhammad, to be the nation's constitution. It is from those sources the government derives its power, not from the people.

As in many absolute monarchies, individual rights are strictly limited in the Kingdom of Saudi Arabia. Among other things, freedom of assembly and expression are restricted by the Basic Law, which states: "All acts that foster sedi-tion [resistance] or division or harm the state's security and its public relations or detract from man's dignity and rights shall be prohibited."[7] In a 2009 report, the human rights organization Amnesty International reported: "Human rights activists and peaceful critics of the government were detained or remained in prison, including prisoners of conscience. Freedom of expression, religion, association, and assembly remained tightly restricted."[8] The government censors academic and cultural events and limits Internet access. Saudi Arabia also dictates Islam as the state religion and the only religion permitted to be practiced openly.

Monarchies that Defy Labels

Some monarchies are difficult to classify as either absolute or nominal. This is because some monarchs are stronger than a nominal head of state yet do not hold all government power. In Tonga, an island nation in the South Pacific, the king controls the votes of a majority of the seats in the parliament, but the people elect the remaining parliament members. The Hashemite Kingdom of Jordan, listed as a constitutional monarchy by the United States Central Intelligence Agency (CIA), has a constitution that concentrates legislative and executive authority with the king, Abdullah II. Its parliament has two chambers, one filled by appointments by the king and the other filled by elections. The king can, and has, dissolved the parliament.

Morocco also has a constitution and an elected parliament, but the constitution places ultimate authority with King Mohammed VI, who can dismiss government ministers, dissolve parliament, call for new elections, and rule by decree. Monaco, in Europe, is a constitutional monarchy in which the reigning prince, Prince Albert II, appoints the government's executive leaders and shares legislative powers with the popularly elected National Council. ⌘

Key Monarchies in World History

Egypt had pharaohs. China had emperors, as did Rome. England had kings and queens. France had kings and emperors. Russia had czars. Throughout the world and throughout history, monarchies have reigned, some for hundreds of years and some for thousands. Many have made their marks on history, for a variety of reasons.

Ancient Egyptian Kings

Monarchy in ancient Egypt is notable for its longevity. Rule by pharaohs began as long ago as 3100 BCE and continued for 3,000 years. Much

King Tutankhamen's mask

of what we know about those ancient kings has been learned through their majestic burial sites, in particular the famous pyramids in Giza. One Egyptian king well-known for his burial ground is Tutankhamen, who ascended to the throne in 1361 BCE. The tomb of Tutankhamen, or King Tut, was discovered in 1922 filled with jewels and other treasures. The discovery of Tut's intact tomb was unusual because grave robbers had looted the tombs of most other ancient Egyptian kings. Tut's tomb also housed the pharaoh's mummified remains. Recent testing of those remains proved Tut was the son and successor of the pharaoh Akhenaton, an important archeological discovery for those looking for proof of dynastic succession.

The last Egyptian pharaoh was a woman, Cleopatra. She ascended the throne in 51 BCE with her brother, but was driven into exile by her brother's supporters. Soon after, the Roman dictator Julius Caesar came to Egypt and helped Cleopatra regain the throne. The two became lovers. After Caesar was assassinated,

THE EGYPTIAN TOMBS

Tens of thousands of Egyptians worked on building the pyramids that served as royal tombs, and the projects took decades to complete. The Egyptians believed that the deceased pharaohs needed their bodies in the afterlife to perform their roles as gods. They thought that disaster would befall Egypt if their monarchs' corpses were not properly cared for and protected after death.

A statue of Julius Caesar stands in Rome, Italy.

Cleopatra became romantically involved with Mark Antony, another Roman ruler. Mark Antony was eventually defeated by Octavian, Caesar's heir, and lost control of Rome. Both Antony and Cleopatra committed suicide, and Egypt became a Roman province.

Rulers of Rome

Julius Caesar is one of the most famous leaders in history. He expanded Rome by conquering many territories, including modern-day France and Turkey. He also led the first Roman invasion of Great Britain. Caesar was appointed dictator following a civil war in Rome. Although not a king, he behaved like one.

Rome had for centuries been a republic, but as Caesar became more popular and more powerful, members of the Roman Senate feared he would declare himself king. A group of conspirators stabbed Caesar to death as he entered the Senate on March 15, 44 BCE. However, Rome never became a republic again. For centuries afterward, it was ruled by a long line of emperors. Rome continued to expand under the emperors' leadership, but in the fifth century, the great empire fell apart. Invading peoples conquered the western part of the empire. The eastern half of the empire continued as the Byzantine Empire, with its capital in Constantinople, modern-day Istanbul, Turkey.

CAESAR'S FAMOUS PHRASE

Julius Caesar's conquest of modern-day Turkey was "so swift," according to historian Richard Hooker, "that Caesar described it in three words: 'Veni, vidi, vici [I came, I saw, I conquered].'"[1]

The Holy Roman Empire

In the Middle Ages, much of Europe was united under Charlemagne, king of the Franks. The Frankish kingdom originally included modern-day

France and other parts of western Europe, but Charlemagne expanded it by conquering the areas that now make up northern Italy and part of Germany. After Charlemagne defeated the Lombards, who were a threat to the Roman Catholic papacy, Pope Leo III crowned Charlemagne emperor of the Romans in 800.

Charlemagne's realm would later become the Holy Roman Empire, which existed in Europe for nearly 1,000 years, beginning with the reign of Otto I in 962 and ending in 1806. Like Charlemagne, the emperors were crowned by the Catholic pope, and therefore were thought of as holy. That practice, however, ended in 1530, and the leaders of the different territories then elected the monarch. Nonetheless, rule tended to be hereditary. The Hapsburg dynasty ruled the Holy Roman Empire for almost 400 years, from the fifteenth century until the empire dissolved in the Napoleonic wars.

Despite its name, the Holy Roman Empire was centered on modern-day Germany, not Rome, and essentially was a German kingship. The empire also included modern-day Austria, the Czech Republic, Switzerland, the Netherlands, Belgium, Luxembourg, and Slovenia, as well as parts of France, Italy, and Poland. In 1756, the philosopher Voltaire commented, "This agglomeration, which was called and which still calls itself the Holy Roman Empire, was neither holy, nor Roman, nor an empire."[2]

Other European Monarchies

Predating the Holy Roman Empire was the British monarchy. It emerged from the Kingdom of Wessex in south-central England and started with the reign of Cerdic in 519 CE. Since then, a number of British monarchs have made their marks on the history of Western civilization. Henry VIII, who ascended the British throne in 1509, is known for having six wives—two of whom were executed at his command. Because the Catholic Church would not allow him to get divorced, he broke with the Catholic pope to found the Church of England. Henry VIII's daughter Elizabeth I became one of the most famous British monarchs. She never married, choosing to reign alone. During her 44-year rule, Britain grew into a powerful empire, defeating an attack by the Spanish Armada in 1588.

In the next century, King Charles I began a feud with Parliament, asserting that he ruled by divine right—meaning by the will of God. Charles I was executed, and England became the English Commonwealth, led by political and military leader Oliver Cromwell. However, the monarchy was restored after Cromwell's death in 1658, when Parliament invited Charles II, son of Charles I, to retake the crown.

When Charles II died, his brother, James II, took the throne. James II was a Roman Catholic, and one of his acts was to bring his religion back to Protestant England, going against Parliament's wishes in doing so. Parliament revolted in what became known as the Glorious Revolution. James II was deposed, and his daughter Mary II, a

Protestant, became queen. Another result of the revolution was the Bill of Rights of 1689, which is considered the basis of England's constitutional monarchy.

As in England, France had a long-lived monarchy, which could trace its roots to the beginning of the Holy Roman Empire. Its longest serving monarch was King Louis XIV, who took the throne in 1643 and reigned for 72 years. During his reign, the palace at Versailles was transformed into an international wonder. His descendant, King Louis XVI, sat on the throne during the French Revolution that began in 1789. He was beheaded, along with his wife, Marie

KINGS OF ANCIENT ISRAEL AND GREECE

Three legendary kings of ancient Israel were Saul, David, and Solomon, said to have ruled beginning around 1030 BCE. The three monarchs' stories are recorded in the Jewish and Christian religious scriptures. Christians believe that Jesus was a descendant of King David.

Alexander the Great is well known as one of the greatest conquerors of ancient times. In 336 BCE, Alexander became king of Macedonia, a part of modern-day Greece. In his twelve-year rule, he built a vast empire that stretched from Greece all the way to western Asia and northern Africa, encompassing the former Persian Empire and Egypt. After Alexander died, his empire was divided among his generals, including Ptolemy, who became king of Egypt and Cleopatra's ancestor.

Russian Czar Peter the Great

Antoinette. Another French monarchy followed soon after, however, when Napoléon I became emperor of France.

In Russia, the monarchy can be traced back to 862. Czar Peter the Great declared the nation to be an empire in 1721. Under Peter, Russia became a world power. Another notable member of the dynasty was Catherine the Great, wife of Czar Peter III. Catherine overthrew her husband in 1762 and ruled for 34 years, during which time Russia's southern border advanced to the Black Sea. The last Russian czar was Nicholas II. Following World War I, a Russian revolution broke out, and Russia came under Communist rule. Nicholas was forced to abdicate, and he and his family were executed.

China's Imperial Dynasties

Dynastic rule in China started at least as far back as the Shang dynasty, which dates to 1766 BCE. That was followed by the Zhou dynasty, which began in 1122 BCE. At that time, power in China was not centralized under one leader. Rather, China operated as a feudal system, divided into various domains headed by princes. However, in 221 BCE, the strongest of the domains, Qin, also known as Ch'in, unified China under the first emperor, Qin Shi Huang. Qin Shi Huang began construction of the Great Wall of China. A centralized bureaucracy with governors and magistrates governing provinces and counties replaced the former system of separately ruled principalities. It became the signature of the nation's imperial dynastic system in centuries to come.

The Yuan, or Mongol, dynasty held power from 1297 to 1368 and marked the first rule of China by non-Chinese people. Kublai Khan, grandson of Mongolian ruler Genghis Khan, was the first emperor of the dynasty. As the Great Khan, or ruler, of Mongolia and the emperor of China, Kublai Khan controlled a vast area that stretched from the Black Sea in Eastern Europe to the Pacific Ocean and from Siberia to Afghanistan.

During the Ming dynasty, which lasted from 1368 to 1644, the Forbidden City was built in Beijing. The enclosed city within a city was the imperial palace used by the Ming and Qing dynasties until the end of the imperial system in 1911. In addition, much of the famous Great Wall of China was built during the Ming dynasty, although parts of it date back to the Qin dynasty in the fifth century BCE. The wall was built in the area of China's northern border to ward off attacks.

Japan's Monarchy

Japan is known for having the oldest continuing hereditary monarchy in the world. Current monarch Emperor Akihito is the one hundred and twenty-fifth Japanese monarch in the line, which may stretch back to 660 BCE. However, a number of the early emperors are considered to be mythical, and some scholars place the beginning of the monarchy at 100 CE to 300 CE.

Unlike other historical monarchs, the Japanese emperors mostly have not been absolute rulers, but rather ceremonial and religious leaders under the control of noble families. For almost a millennium, political and military power in Japan has been in the hands of shoguns, or military leaders. Imperial rule returned in the late 1800s. However, when Japan was defeated in World War II, Emperor Hirohito had to give up much of his power. Akihito, his son, consequently handled only ceremonial duties in the country. ⌘

4

The Origins and Expansion of Power

Ninth-century ruler Kenneth MacAlpin is known as the founder of the Scottish monarchy. MacAlpin was the son of King Alpin of Dalriada, a Celt society that moved its base from Ireland to western Scotland around 500 CE. Yet another earlier leader was in charge of that move—a tribal chief named Fergus.

Sixteenth century ruler Ivan IV, also known as Ivan the Terrible, is considered the first Russian czar. However, he is not the first Russian monarch

Russian Czar Ivan IV

IVAN THE TERRIBLE.

to be called czar and certainly not the first Russian monarch. Ivan IV was a grand prince of Moscow, just like his father, Vasilii. And Ivan III, who unified Russia and was an ancestor of Ivan IV, also was called czar. Still, the monarchy did not start there. Monarchial rule in Russia has been traced back as far as Rurik, a Viking warrior whose rule of a portion of Russia is dated to around 862 CE.

In the twentieth century, King Abdul Aziz Al Saud founded the Kingdom of Saudi Arabia. But he was not the first ruler from the Saud family. He succeeded his father, Abdul Rahman ibn Faisal, as sultan of Nejd, the central region of Saudi Arabia. Saud family rule in Saudi Arabia can be traced back to the early eighteenth century. At that time, Muhammad ibn Saud, a politician and warrior, allied himself with Muhammad ibn-Abdul Wahhab, a reformer of the Islam religion, to create the first Saudi state. But the earliest recorded Saud ancestor goes back to the fifteenth century, to Mani' ibn Rabi'ah al-Muraydi, who settled in an area near the present-day Saudi Arabian capital of Riyadh given to him by another ruler, known as ibn Dir.

Monarchies Born of Tribal Conflict

Monarchies commonly evolved from tribal rule by chiefs. When the chiefs warred with one another, the loser would cede to the winner his territory, which might include important trade routes or fertile land. In this way, certain tribal chiefs acquired more power and territory, which was then passed down to their offspring. The ruling clan continued to consolidate power and territory, but the warring continued as they were always vulnerable to power grabs from others.

In England, Celtic tribes existed for millennia before the Christian era. Roman troops conquered them in ancient times, but when the Romans left in 408 CE, the tribes remained. Invaders from what is now Germany and Scandinavia came to Britain, taking over Celtic kingdoms and creating new ones. The smaller kingdoms fell to the more powerful, and eventually there were seven small kingdoms that were all absorbed by the Kingdom of Wessex. This begat the British monarchy that holds the crown today.

Monarchies Born of Necessity and Progress

Monarchy in many cases arose from a need to bring order and necessary services and infrastructure to societies that were becoming more complex. Sumer, one of the earliest civilizations in the world, is an example. It was established in Mesopotamia, a swath of land between the Tigris and Euphrates Rivers in modern-day Iraq. Originally, Sumerians had tribal rule, in which the chief of the tribe was the head of the family. Tribes would fight each other, with the winner taking over the loser. Eventually, city-states that had 10,000 residents or more were formed.

With so many people, organization was needed. Priests, who became priest-kings, emerged as leaders. At first, the priest-kings were thought to be divinely chosen. Later, the leaders were considered to be divine themselves. Because the priest-king ruled over a large territory and many people, a bureaucracy formed to provide management help. One of the tasks facing the priest-king and his government was the distribution of food. Now that the society was no longer made up only of farmers, city dwellers needed help getting food from the countryside.

Similarly, in ancient Egypt, where an agricultural society arose around the Nile River, the monarchy managed irrigation systems necessary for productive farming. Irrigation helped create new farmland out of previously unsuitable land.

KING LOUIS XIV AND GOD

Louis XIV, the king of France from 1643 to 1715, embraced the doctrine of divine right of kings as the basis for absolute power. He said, "It is legal because I wish it."[1] He also remarked, *"L'etat c'est moi,"* which means: "The state, it is I."[2]

Power Won Through Warfare

Once monarchies were established, they often turned to warfare for conquering and defense. By conquering other lands, monarchs acquired natural and human resources that could bring more money and strength to the kingdom. Monarchial conquests can be charted throughout

Alexander the Great

human history, from ancient civilizations through the twentieth century.

In 331 BCE, King Alexander the Great of Macedonia conquered Egypt and the Persian Empire. His reign went as far as India. Octavian, who became the first Roman emperor under the name Caesar Augustus in 27 BCE, conquered and annexed Egypt to the Roman Empire. His armies also conquered what are now Spain and Portugal and some parts of Germany by the time of his death in 14 CE. In the eighth century, King Charlemagne of the Franks led more than 50 military campaigns that led to his realm covering what are now France, Switzerland, the Netherlands, Belgium, and parts of Italy, Germany,

Austria, and Spain. In the thirteenth century, Mongolian Emperor Kublai Khan gained control of China, establishing a dynasty there. When Kublai Khan died in 1294, his territory covered 22 percent of the world's land area. The Ottoman Empire began in a small territory in Anatolia in what is now western Turkey. With conquests spanning the next several hundred years, it amassed territory that included parts of Africa, Asia, and Europe. Some of the modern-day countries that were once wholly or partially part of the Ottoman Empire include Algeria, Sudan, and Libya in Africa; Jordan, Lebanon, Oman, Qatar, Syria, Yemen, and Saudi Arabia in Asia; and the Balkan states, Greece, and Cyprus in Europe. At the end of the eighteenth century and the beginning of the nineteenth century, Napoléon I conquered much of Western Europe to create a French empire, and he became its emperor.

As recently as the twentieth century, monarchs have used military might to consolidate power. In 1902, Abdul

EUROPE'S BIG ROYAL FAMILY

Marriages arranged among royal families in Europe over the centuries mean several of today's European monarchs are related to each other. Even Queen Elizabeth II is a distant relative of her husband, Prince Philip, a former Greek prince. The two are great-great-grandchildren of England's Queen Victoria. So are Queen Margrethe of Denmark and King Juan Carlos I of Spain. Queen Margrethe and King Harald V of Norway are both great-grandchildren of King Frederick VIII of Denmark.

Aziz Al Saud, a member of the Saud family that previously ruled portions of the Arabian Peninsula, successfully attacked Riyadh and attracted followers. He created a force of Islamic warriors and expelled the Rashid ruling family from the Najd region surrounding Riyadh. In addition to the Najd, King Abdul Aziz controlled central Arabia. In the mid-1920s, he invaded the Hijaz, the western part of the Arabian Peninsula where the Islamic holy cities of Mecca and Medina stand. The move forced the abdication of Hussein bin Ali, who had claimed the title of king of Arab Lands in 1916. The British recognized King Abdul Aziz as king of the Hijaz and sultan of Najd. By the early 1930s, the king expanded his rule to more of the Arabian Peninsula, and in 1932 he named his territory the Kingdom of Saudi Arabia.

Love, Not War

While monarchies frequently expanded their power base through conquest, they often protected it by less bloody means: through marriage. Members of royal families in one country often would marry members of royal families in other countries to forge alliances. It was a common way to neutralize threats.

King Henry I ascended the English throne in 1100 and married Matilda, the daughter of the king of Scots, approximately 500 years before England and Scotland joined as a single kingdom. Henry was of Norman French descent—the son of William, the Duke of Normandy who had conquered England in 1066. Matilda was a princess of Anglo-Saxon descent. By joining the Norman and Anglo-Saxon royal families, Henry aimed to consolidate his position as king of England and Duke of Normandy.

FAMILY FEUDS

The interrelationship among European royalty created awkward situations during World War I. King George V, the king of Great Britain, was a cousin of Kaiser Wilhelm II, the German emperor. Britain and Germany were on opposite sides of the war, making the cousins enemies.

Another cousin, Alexandra, was married to Czar Nicholas II of Russia, a British ally in World War I. Following the war, Nicholas was overthrown by a popular revolution. George V planned to offer asylum to his cousin, but he changed his mind when British public opinion seemed to turn against the idea. Russian revolutionaries later executed the czar and czarina and their family.

Henry II, who ruled England from 1154 to 1189, married the daughter of the Duke of Aquitaine in France and therefore had dominion over that territory in addition to rule over Normandy, which he inherited. Edward III became king of England in 1327 and later claimed to be the king of France because his mother was the daughter of France's King Louis IV. This declaration led to war, however, as the French did not recognize his claim to their throne. England fought France for more than 100 years in a futile attempt to gain the throne. Nonetheless, England's monarchs until 1801 claimed the title of French king. In the sixteenth century, Queen Mary I, half Spanish and a Catholic, married King

Philip II of Spain, also a Catholic, to shield herself from Protestants who wanted to oust her.

In continental Europe in the eighteenth century, the marriage of Marie Antoinette, daughter of the Holy Roman emperor, to France's King Louis XVI was arranged to create an alliance between France and Austria, the seat of the Holy Roman Empire. In the nineteenth century, Queen Victoria of England married off her nine children to royalty throughout Europe. ⌘

5

Staying in Power

Kings have not fared well in Asia. In China, India, Mongolia, and elsewhere, monarchies have been abolished by various means, including revolution. That did not escape the notice of the residents of Bhutan, a tiny Asian country in the Himalayan Mountains. Bhutan's transition from an absolute monarchy to a parliamentary system has been a slow process that began in the mid-1950s. "The region has seen bad endings for kings. It's something the Bhutanese wanted to avoid," a Western diplomat observed.[1]

With this in mind, the kings of Bhutan, who exercised absolute rule since the first one was seated in 1907, embarked on a course leading to

Bhutan's King Jigme Khesar Namgyal Wangchuk, left, walks with his father and the fourth king, Jigme Singye Wangchuck, in 2008.

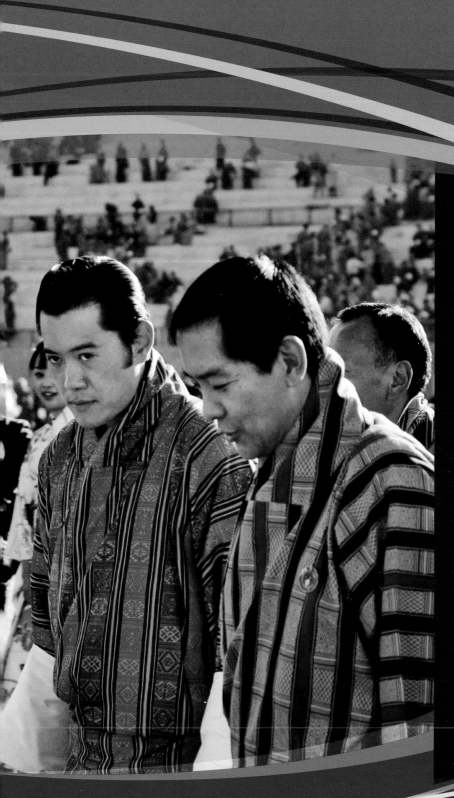

democracy. The National Assembly was established in 1953, and the king relinquished his veto powers. In 1968, the National Assembly gained the ability to remove the sovereign, and regional governing bodies were created in the 1980s and 1990s. In 1999, the fourth king, Jigme Singye Wangchuk, created the Council of Ministers to exercise executive power, while the king retained the largely ceremonial position of head of state.

During a December 17, 2005, address to mark National Day, the anniversary of the day Ugyen Wangchuk became Bhutan's first hereditary monarch in 1907, the king announced that the first elections for a new, bicameral parliament would be held by 2008. He also planned to abdicate in favor of his eldest son, Jigme Khesar Namgyal Wangchuk. The king said:

> After 26 years of the process of decentralization and devolution of powers to the people, I have every confidence that our people will be able to choose the best political party that can provide good governance and serve the interest of the nation.[2]

As promised, elections were held. The government was formed, the king abdicated, and his son was crowned. However, the people of Bhutan had been content with their leader and were not overjoyed by the change, according to a report in Britain's the *Independent*. "No one wants this election," Yeshi Zimba, one of the candidates in the 2008 election, told the *Independent*. "His Majesty has guided us this far, and people are asking, 'Why change now?'"[3]

But the king had his reasons. By handing power to the people while at the same time handing down the throne to his son, the king kept the hereditary monarchy alive while leaving the people little reason to follow the revolutionary routes other countries had taken.

Transfer of Power in Constitutional Monarchies

As in Bhutan, constitutional monarchies that formerly were absolute monarchies have been able to stay in power, or at least stay in place, by virtue of political power shifting from royalty to the people and to elected politicians. Before, when kings ruled absolutely, the people could point to the crown for causing, or failing to resolve, their discontent. Under a constitutional monarchy, problems are laid at the feet of the democratically elected government, which makes the decisions, rather than at the feet of the king or queen, whose role is largely ceremonial.

"The institution of monarchy, far from being an anachronistic relic, is finding new justifications: as a unifying force for increasingly diverse populations and as a national symbol at a time when other representations of identity—like border controls and currencies—are being subsumed in the larger concept of Europe."[4]

—Aisha Labi, journalist, Time *magazine*

In England, Queen Elizabeth II opens Parliament by reading a speech written by the governing political party, appoints the prime minister by giving the position to the leader of the party that won the most seats in the House of Commons in the most recent election, signs legislation into law by giving royal assent, and dissolves Parliament when the prime minister tells her to do so. In Japan, the emperor has no governmental role and is seen largely as a national symbol. Nonetheless, the emperor still holds the throne, and his son and grandson are in line to take over when he dies.

The possibility exists that even these seemingly nonthreatening monarchies could be eliminated by their governments should the citizens decide royalty is superfluous. Staying in place, then, is a matter of convincing citizens the institution is relevant; that is, that a monarchy is not obsolete or out of date

MAINTAINING THE STATUS QUO

While he was a prince in 1894 studying the English constitution, Britain's King George V wrote the following in his study notes: "The existence of the crown serves to disguise change and therefore to deprive it of the evil consequences of revolution."[5] His statement suggests the monarchy's role in making things appear to continue as they always have, even as they are actually changing, is the way it protects itself from being eliminated.

but a worthwhile institution that puts the nation in a positive light and helps engender feelings of national pride. To help win public approval, monarchs often help with charitable causes, preside over ceremonies, and make overseas visits as their nations' representatives. King George V, who ruled the United Kingdom from 1910 to 1936, is an example. British biographer Miranda Carter wrote of King George V's activities:

> *The King and his secretaries believed the British royal family must sell itself to the nation, justify its existence and seem entirely unthreatening. George threw himself into the project, steeling himself to appear more in public while hating every moment; making radio broadcasts that made him sick with nerves; endlessly visiting poorer industrial regions, turning the adoption of philanthropic projects into a royal industry.[6]*

The British monarchy continues in that fashion today, with members of the royal family working on behalf of numerous philanthropic causes. Furthermore, Queen Elizabeth II has traveled extensively both to Commonwealth countries and to nations outside the Commonwealth during her more than 50-year reign. The tours have made her popular.

By making the international rounds and by acting as national symbols within their countries, the monarchs tap into the public's feelings of nationalism. This is another way they stay relevant. Efforts by some monarchs, such as King Juan Carlos I of Spain and King Albert II of Belgium, to keep their countries from being

King Louis XIV of France

pulled apart by internal factions also may prove the monarchies' power and value.

Fostering Allegiance and Creating Allies

Traditionally, monarchs in Europe held on to their power with the help of the nobility or upper class. The monarchs awarded land, wealth, and privileges in exchange for support. This contributed to great inequality among the classes. Before the French Revolution, for example, the French nobility did not have to pay taxes, which helped members of that privileged class hold onto their wealth while they collected rent and dues from peasants. The nobility also populated the government bureaucracy, which enabled them to exercise considerable power. In England, the nobles were the first members of Parliament, where they advised the monarchs and also exercised some influence upon them.

Monarchs also stayed in power by trying to manage external threats through marriage. Princes and princesses from one country routinely married princes and princesses from another to form alliances and to guard against invasion.

Power from God

Another means monarchs have used to both acquire power and to protect it is to claim it was given to them divinely. The theory was that certain kings received their power from God, so they were not answerable to humans and, therefore, should rule absolutely. The idea that they were divinely chosen lent legitimacy to their rule and helped them stay in power. It also negated influence by nobles, who held power in the medieval feudal system, and by organized religions such as the Roman Catholic Church, which also had influence on monarchs. In medieval France, the Roman Catholic Church anointed kings, reinforcing their legitimacy. King Louis XIV of France articulated the divine right theory in the

Japan's Emperor Hirohito, 1918

seventeenth century. Charles I, who ruled Britain
in the seventeenth century, also espoused the
theory, much to the unhappiness of Parliament.
He was eventually executed for treason.

The idea of divine right is an ancient one. Monarchs in ancient Japan, Egypt, and Sumer were considered divine. Japanese legend has it that the country's first emperor, Jimmu, who is said to have ruled in 660 BCE, was descended from the sun goddess. In 1946, following Japan's loss in World War II, Emperor Hirohito renounced his monarchy's divinity. Hirohito declared that relations between the ruler and his people could not be based on "the false conception that the emperor is divine or that the Japanese people are superior to other races."[7] Nonetheless, some traditional Japanese still view their emperor as more than an ordinary human being. "The emperor is a special existence," said Yuko Tojo, granddaughter of Japanese wartime leader Tojo Hideki. "He is not like normal people. The idea that he is a symbol of Japan as we have been taught

OUSTING ONE OF THEIR OWN

Sometimes popular revolutions unseat kings, but other times the revolution comes from within, as power is transferred forcefully within the royal house. That is what happened in Saudi Arabia in 1964 during the rule of King Saud. The royal family, unhappy with King Saud's handling of national finances and foreign affairs, made him hand over government management to Prince Faisal, next in line to the throne. King Saud took back control after a couple of years but was ultimately forced by a decree from religious leaders to abdicate in favor of Prince Faisal.

in the postwar period is insulting. He is the essence of Japan."[8]

Holding onto Power in Arab Monarchies

While handing power off to the people and fostering a role as a national symbol of unity has helped some European monarchies hold onto power, different forces are at work in the Arab world. There, the monarchies are strong or absolute, rather than nominal. A number of those societies have tribal cultures with dynastic chiefs, so the idea of a national government headed by a king and his family fits into cultural expectations.

The Saudi government is more like an oligarchy, in which a group of powerful people rule, than an absolute monarchy with rule by one person. In Saudi Arabia, the ruling family is the power behind the throne. The family is quite large because the men can have more than one wife and, consequently, many children. Consensus among ruling family members factors into the government. The ruling family also seeks consensus from sectors of the governed. For example, when King Saud was forced out and one of his brothers, King Faisal, was elevated to the throne in the 1960s, the proclamation of Faisal as king came not only from the royal family but also from religious leaders. As Anthony H. Cordesman, an expert on national security, wrote in his book, *Saudi Arabia Enters the Twenty-First Century*:

Saudi monarchs have long recognized that they must maintain the support of senior members of the Saudi royal family, as well as the support of the Ulema [religious leadership], leading technocrats, key businessmen, regional and tribal leaders and other important elements in Saudi society. As in other Southern Gulf countries, the king and royal family must also be accessible to the people.[9]

As Cordesman mentioned, religion is another factor in the Saudi king's ability to hold onto power. The king must observe Islamic law, and the Islamic clergy ensures it is enforced in the land. The descendants of Muhammad ibn-Abdul Wahhab, the spiritual leader with whom the Saud family allied itself when it first acquired power in the eighteenth century, also influence the Saudi government.

RESTRICTIONS IN JORDAN

In Jordan, the constitution supposedly protects speech and press freedoms, but in practice these freedoms are severely limited. Publications must be licensed by the state, and journalists are subject to vague laws and censorship. In 2008, Fayez al-Ajrashi, editor of the weekly newspaper *El-Ekhbariya,* was arrested and detained for several days before being charged with "inciting sectarian strife" and "sowing national discord."[10] The case stemmed from articles he wrote that criticized the governor of Amman, Jordan's capital city, and dealt with corruption there.

Using Power to Keep Power

Absolute monarchies sometimes keep their power by stifling opposition. By restricting freedom of speech and freedom of the press, any views that are unsympathetic to the rulers are not disseminated, unlike views that are supportive of the regime. When freedom of assembly is restricted, groups cannot legally organize or rally against the existing regime.

In its 2009 Human Rights Report on Saudi Arabia, the United States Department of State noted the kingdom's restrictions of speech, assembly, and press freedom. It also noted the government's lack of transparency, meaning that the public is neither part of nor able to view the government's decision-making process. Saudi Arabia also arrests and imprisons human rights activists and peaceful critics of the government, according to Amnesty International, a human-rights watchdog group.

Saudi Arabia is not alone in restricting freedoms to guard against dissent. The US State Department reported restrictions on freedom of speech, press, and assembly in the Kingdom of Swaziland, where it noted harassment of journalists, prohibitions on political activity, and harassment of political activists. The governments in Jordan, the United Arab Emirates, Oman, and Qatar also restrict civil liberties, including access to the Internet.

To survive, monarchies must retain power in some form. For constitutional monarchies, giving away political power has allowed monarchs to retain their sovereignty, even if it is simply ceremonial. Among the absolute monarchies, seeking consensus and quashing dissent are the means by which they keep power in their hands. ⌘

6

Succession in Monarchies

Elizabeth II became sovereign of the United Kingdom and Commonwealth realms when her father died. When she dies, her eldest son, Prince Charles, will inherit the throne and become king. When Charles dies, his eldest son, William, will become king, and so on.

Monarchy often is hereditary, which means the position is passed down within a family, usually from one generation to the next. Things do not always go as planned, however. Kings and queens do not always have children, or male children, who have been preferred in the lines of

Prince Charles is next in the line of succession in the United Kingdom.

royal succession. Therefore, the line of succession is sometimes stretched. For example, after Queen Elizabeth I of England died without heirs, King James VI of Scotland, the great-great-grandson of Henry VII of England, became England's King James I.

Sometimes the line of succession is broken. At the beginning of the nineteenth century, King Charles XIII of Sweden had no surviving child, so the Swedish parliament offered in 1810 to make a popular French military marshal, Jean Baptiste Bernadotte, the heir. He became King Charles XIV John in 1818. As a result, the Swedish royal house is called the House of Bernadotte.

The glitches that arose when transferring sovereignty by custom from one monarch to the next led nations to codify rules of succession. The Act of Settlement of 1701 was passed by the British Parliament to ensure only Protestants could become monarch. That is because the monarch

KING GEORGE I

The Act of Settlement of 1701 was established to prevent Catholic claimants from ascending the British throne. However, the search for a suitable Protestant ruler sometimes meant going outside of England. For instance, Sophia of Hanover, a Protestant granddaughter of James I, was named as the successor of Queen Anne. When Sophia died before Anne did, Sophia's son George became heir to the throne and later King George I of England. George had lived his entire life in Hanover, in present-day Germany, and could hardly speak any English.

is head of the Protestant Church of England in addition to being head of state. Specifically, the act prohibits Roman Catholics and anyone married to a Roman Catholic from becoming king or queen. The rule prohibiting Roman Catholics on the throne continues to this day. King George V's grandson Prince Michael of Kent and great-grandson George Windsor both forfeited their places in the line of succession by marrying Roman Catholics.

Preference for Male Heirs

Monarchial succession often favors male heirs. It is a practice that stems from the system of primogeniture in the feudal era, when the eldest child inherited the entirety of an estate to the exclusion of other siblings and relatives. Male descendants took precedence over female descendants. In royal succession in modern times, some monarchies, such as England, have

TIME FOR A FEMALE EMPEROR?

Japan has a long history of only allowing males to ascend to the throne. Crown Prince Naruhito will succeed his father as emperor, but because his only child is a daughter, for years his successor was in question. A government panel issued a proposal that Princess Aiko be allowed to ascend the throne after her father and recommended that in the future gender not be a factor in succession. The change would have reduced the uncertainty about the continuance of the royal line. However, the recommendation was dropped when Naruhito's younger brother had a son, Prince Hisahito. It was determined that the young prince would succeed his uncle.

male preference primogeniture. Male heirs are first in line, but women are not prohibited from taking the throne. For example, Britain's George VI had two daughters, so the throne went to Elizabeth, the eldest of the two. But if George VI had had a son, even one younger than Elizabeth, he would have ascended the throne. In another example, Elizabeth II's daughter, Anne, is older than her brothers, Andrew and Edward, but she comes after them and their children in the line of succession. Spain and Monaco also use male preference primogeniture.

In Japan, the law provides for male emperors only. The son of Emperor Akihito, Crown Prince Naruhito, and his wife, Crown Princess Masako, have a daughter, not a son. Even though Naruhito will one day be emperor, his child will not. Instead, the crown will pass to Prince Hisahito, the son of Naruhito's brother Prince Akishino. The pressure to produce a male heir reportedly placed tremendous stress upon Crown Princess Masako. The princess, a former diplomat who was educated at Harvard University in the United States and Oxford University in England, suspended her public duties due to mental illness caused by the stress of royal life, which included the pressure to bear a son. "She may be rather happy to be off the hook from the mountain of pressure on her only daughter, Aiko," said Sayo Miyazaki, a school clerk in Japan at the time of Prince Hisahito's birth.[1]

Succession Rules Change

Five European monarchies have changed their succession rules since 1980 to eliminate male favoritism in succession. Sweden, the Netherlands, Norway, Belgium, and Denmark now practice equal primogeniture, also known as absolute primogeniture or fully cognatic primogeniture. It means the eldest heir, regardless of gender, inherits the throne. Similar change has been considered by other nations, including the United Kingdom. There, the government said it planned to give equal rights to princesses as well as to eliminate the ban on heirs to the throne marrying Roman Catholics. Polls showed the public favored the changes, but the government

THE PRETENDERS

Although it may seem orderly, succession is often unruly. Throughout history, kings have abdicated or were thrown out, people seized the throne from rightful claimants, governments changed the rules of succession without the royal family's input, or monarchies were abolished altogether. As a result of all this confusion, there have often been multiple people claiming the throne really belongs to them. A person with a claim to a throne he or she does not hold, whether their claim is legitimate or not, is called a pretender. A number of these pretenders to the throne were alive throughout Europe in 2010, including Vittorio Emanuele, the last crown prince of Italy; Constantine II, the last king of Greece; and Simeon II of Bulgaria, who lost his throne following World War II and was exiled by the communists who took over his country. When communism fell to democracy, Simeon ran successfully for Bulgaria's parliament and served as prime minister from 2001 to 2005.

has not followed through. The Attorney General's Department released a statement:

> *To bring about changes to the law on succession would be a complex undertaking involving amendment or repeal of a number of items of related legislation, as well as requiring the consent of legislatures of member nations of the Commonwealth. We are of course ready to consider the arguments in this area but there are no immediate plans to legislate.*[2]

In Monaco, the reigning monarch is Prince Albert. However, since he is yet unmarried and has no children, the parliament changed the succession rules in 2002 to allow his sisters' sons to take the throne if Albert never had a legitimate child. Albert did father two children out of wedlock, but children born outside of marriage are not eligible to inherit the throne in the Catholic principality. Albert may yet produce an heir, as the 52-year-old monarch announced in June 2010 that he planned to marry his 32-year-old girlfriend, Charlene Wittstock.

Japan began considering whether to allow women to ascend the emperor's throne earlier this century, but the matter became less urgent following the 2006 birth of Prince Hisahito. Still, it may be revisited. Junichiro Koizumi, who was Japan's prime minister when the prince was born, said, "It will be difficult to maintain the imperial family system without allowing females to ascend to the throne."[3]

Succession by Vote

While heredity is the main method of succession, some monarchs ascend the throne by election. Such is the case for the Roman Catholic pope, who is elected by cardinals—the highest-ranking clergymen of the church—to lifetime leadership of the church as well as the Vatican City nation-state. Any male Roman Catholic can be elected, but the position has gone only to cardinals for more than six centuries.

In Andorra, a tiny co-principality that borders France and Spain, an elected prince and an appointed prince are coheads of state. The elected prince, or lay prince, is the president of France, who is elected by the French voters for a five-year term. The other, the so-called episcopal prince, is the bishop of Seu d'Argell of Spain, an appointed position within the Roman Catholic Church. When the president of France changes as a

ANDORRA

Andorra is a tiny nation half the size of New York City tucked between Spain and France with the unique status of co-principality, in which two princes serve as head of state. Created by Charlemagne in 800 BCE, rule was later passed to the Count of Urgell in Spain, then to the Roman Catholic Diocese of Urgell. Later, the bishop of the diocese, worried about military attacks, placed himself under the protection of a Spanish nobleman. When a French count became an heir to the Spanish nobleman, a dispute arose over Andorra between the county and the Spanish bishop. In 1278, the problem was solved by giving sovereignty to both the count and the bishop.

result of French elections, or when the bishop of Seu d'Argell changes as the result of an appointment, the princes change as well.

In Cambodia, the king is chosen by the Royal Council of the Throne, which includes the nation's prime minister and other political leaders as well as chiefs from two orders of Buddhist monks. The reigning monarch cannot choose his heir, and the heir need not be a direct descendant, although he must be a member of the royal family. Those considered by the council for succession must be males 30 years of age or older who are descended from the bloodline of King Ang Duong, who ruled in the mid-nineteenth century, or from one of Ang Duong's sons, King Norodom or King Sisowoth. When King Norodom Sihanouk abdicated in 2004, his son Norodom Sihamoni succeeded him.

In Malaysia, which is a federation of states, the nominal king-sultan is elected by and from the hereditary rulers of nine of the nation's eleven provinces to a five-year term. The principle of rotation is followed as a new ruler is elected every five years. Similarly, in the United Arab Emirates, the president of the federation is chosen for a five-year term by and from among the absolute rulers of the seven federation emirates who convene as the Supreme Council. However, the roles of both president, which is the head of state, and prime minister, which is the head of government, are hereditary in practice.

Japanese Crown Prince Naruhito with his wife, Crown Princess Masako, and their daughter, Princess Aiko, in 2009

Hereditary Monarchies, with a Catch

In Lesotho in Africa, the monarchy is hereditary, but a college of chiefs can elect or depose the monarch by a majority vote and decide who is next in line of succession. In Bhutan in Asia, the national assembly can remove the monarch with a two-thirds vote.

Saudi Arabia's 1992 constitution stipulates the monarch must be a son or grandchild of King Abdul Aziz Al Saud, the founder of the kingdom, and that the reigning king decides who his successor will be. So far, those kings all have been sons of the founding king, who had 34 sons by 17 of his 22 wives. Traditionally, succession was based on seniority, with eldest sons acceding the throne followed by next eldest. An informal decision-making body legitimizes royal succession. The group has about 100 members from the ruling family and ally families as well as religious leaders and commoners.

In 2007, an Allegiance Commission of Saudi princes was established to play a role in succession, but it will not take effect until Crown Prince Sultan becomes king. Under the Allegiance Commission rules, the reigning king will send three nominees to the Allegiance Commission, which will elect one as the crown prince, or heir. Or, the commission can reject the king's nominees and elect a nominee of its own, who can be rejected by the king, leading to a sort of run-off election.

LESOTHO

The Kingdom of Lesotho is a landlocked African country bordered on all sides by South Africa. The United Kingdom recognized Lesotho as a nation headed by tribal chief Moshoeshoe I in 1843. The nation subsequently became a British colony but became independent in 1966 under the rule of King Moshoeshoe II, the father of the current monarch, King Letsie III. Many of Lesotho's citizens are economically disadvantaged. More than half of the almost 2 million residents are considered poor, according to Lesotho statistics from 2002–2003, and 22.5 percent were unemployed in 2008. More than 80 percent of the citizens are subsistence farmers; that is, they grow food for their own consumption.

The winner would become crown prince. The commission also can step in to offer the kingship to the crown prince if it determines the king is incapable of exercising his powers. Still, Simon Henderson of the Washington Institute for New East Policy noted, "Under the new system, as under the old, Saudi policymaking is an exclusively royal prerogative."[4] ⌘

7

How Monarchies End

Nepal is known as the home of Mount Everest, the world's tallest mountain. In 2008, it also became the world's newest republic after a constituent assembly voted to end more than 200 years of royal rule. "I am overjoyed," student Rajesh Subedi, 21, said as people in the nation's capital of Kathmandu celebrated the vote on May 28 of that year. "This is the most important day of my life."[1]

The vote was part of a chain of events that began when the Communist Party of Nepal, also known as the Maoists, launched a civil war in

Members of the Constituent Assembly cheer as the monarchy is abolished and Nepal is declared a republic on May 28, 2008.

1996 to end what was a constitutional monarchy and replace it with a socialist republic. Citing the need to put down the insurgency, King Gyanendra took on absolute power for himself in February 2005. "This will restore peace and effective democracy in this country within the next three years," the king said at the time.[2]

Perhaps in a way he had not intended, the king was correct. Later in 2005, the Maoists and other political parties agreed upon a plan intended to restore democracy. In April 2006, public protests forced King Gyanendra to restore the nation's parliament, and the following month, the parliament voted unanimously to curtail the king's power. In April 2008, a new assembly was elected that included the Maoists and other political parties. In May 2008, the vote to end the monarchy was one of the assembly's first acts.

THOUGHTS ON NEPAL

Journalist Ashis Chakrabarti, who reported on the dissolution of the monarchy in Nepal in 2008, wrote: "Having witnessed the latest events in Nepal, I am convinced one more time that the people's age is well and truly here and kings and emperors are anachronisms today."[3]

Revolutions

As in Nepal, a monarchy can end through revolution, which is the complete change of a government in a short period of time.

Revolutions are brought about within the country rather than imposed upon it. The entire structure and type of government changes; it is not just a change of the people holding office. The instrument of revolution can be the people as a whole or a segment of the population, such as a group with a particular political philosophy.

Revolutions instigated by the people who live under a monarchy have typically sought to replace that form of government with a republic. A republic is a system of government with no monarch. Rather, representatives elected by the people hold political power.

The French Revolution

One of the world's most famous revolutions happened at the end of the eighteenth century in France, which was ruled by King Louis XVI. Government debt led the king and his ministers to try to raise money by taxing the nobles and clergy. However, the nobles and clergy resisted the reforms. Seeking a solution, the king convened the Estates General, an assembly of representatives from the clergy,

PEACEFUL ENDS

A couple of monarchies that died in the wake of World War II did so peacefully, as the result of votes and not bullets. Italy abolished its monarchy in 1946 following a referendum in which the majority of voters favored a republic. Hungary's monarchy was abolished the same year by a vote of parliament, similar to the action taken in 2008 in Nepal.

the nobility, and the commoners. A solution to the fiscal problems was not forthcoming, however. Instead, the commoners broke away from the convention and formed the National Assembly. When the king decreed acts undertaken by the National Assembly to be void, the civilians armed themselves and, on July 14, 1789, set upon the Bastille, a prison in Paris. One reason was to seize gunpowder they believed was stored there, but the attack on the Bastille was also symbolic. "The Bastille was widely hated as a symbol of ministerial despotism," wrote historian George Rude.[4] A gunfight broke out, and the Bastille fell under the crowd's control. To this day, July 14 is celebrated as Bastille Day in France.

After taking control of France, the National Assembly created a constitution. France would now be ruled as a constitutional monarchy. Louis XVI was to remain on the throne as the hereditary king of France, but without absolute power.

THE LOST KING

After his father's beheading in 1793, eight-year-old Louis Charles, son of Louis XVI and Marie Antoinette, was to be king of France but never ruled. Royal records state that Louis Charles died two years later in a prison cell of tuberculosis, but for two centuries doubts existed about his fate. Some people questioned whether royalists had helped the real Louis Charles to escape, leaving a substitute boy to die in prison. In the decades following, several different men claimed to be or were believed by others to be the real Louis Charles. In 2000, the mystery was solved when scientists compared DNA from the heart of the boy who died in prison to a lock of hair belonging to Marie Antoinette and found a match.

Instead, the unicameral National Assembly was to hold the power. Titles and hereditary nobility were abolished, and the aristocracy ended.

Louis XVI resisted governmental changes, however, and tried to flee France with his family. When this failed, the king's powers were revoked in 1792. France became a republic without a monarchy, with the National Assembly holding governmental power. Louis was convicted of treason for scheming against the revolution. He was beheaded on January 21, 1793. "I forgive those who are guilty of my death, and I pray God that the blood which you are about to shed may never be required of France," Louis said before his execution.[5] Following the beheading, "the people were silent for a moment, as though stunned by the shock of the spectacle," author Christopher Hibbert wrote. "Then they began to cry, *'Vive la Nation!' 'Vive la République!'*"[6]

But, the original republic did not live long. France experienced several changes in government following the French Revolution, including the restoration of the monarchy. However, the country eventually returned to republican government, which exists today.

The Monarchial Casualties of World War I

Several monarchy governments, some of which dated back many centuries were overturned in favor of republics as recently as the beginning of the last century. Most of those monarchies dissolved as the result of revolutions that happened in the wake of World War I, which lasted from 1914 to 1918. Among them were the Austro-Hungarian Empire (created from Austria and Hungary in the mid-1800s), the Russian Empire, the Ottoman Empire, and the German Empire.

World War I began with the assassination of the Archduke Franz Ferdinand, heir to the throne of Austria-Hungary. Ferdinand was killed by Bosnian-Serb nationalists who opposed their homeland's annexation to the empire. In response to the assassination, the Austro-Hungarian Empire, backed by its ally Germany, declared war on the nation of Serbia. Russia allied with Serbia. The Ottoman Empire entered the fray in opposition to Russia. France and Britain joined on Russia's side, along with Italy and the United States.

When it became clear Austria-Hungary was going to be on the losing side of the war, its Romanian and Slavic national minorities declared independence from the empire. Austria and Hungary became republics, and the ruling Hapsburg family was exiled. Karl I, Franz Ferdinand's son and heir, gave up power, never to regain the throne.

The Ottoman Empire was another casualty of the war. It began around 1300 as a Muslim state in a part of present-day Turkey and expanded to include large swaths of Europe, Asia, and Africa. Its rulers, called sultans, were considered absolute, although a large bureaucracy that actually ran the government also held a lot of power. In addition to leading the empire, the sultans also held the title of caliph, or supreme spiritual leader of Islam. The empire went through a long period of decline and secessions. By the conclusion of World War I, the empire was reduced to Turkey alone. "The great Empire, the great Caliphate that stood as a lion before the advancing mercantile and military expansion against Europe, slowly crumbled under European pressure," wrote historian Richard Hooker in his history of the Ottoman Empire.[7] After World War I, reformists revolted against the monarchist Ottoman government. The sultanate was abolished, and the Republic of Turkey was founded in 1923.

The Russian monarchy also fell as a result of internal revolution at the end of World War I. As was the case with the Ottoman Empire, the Russian empire was very large and diverse, making it difficult to rule. It was ruled by an absolute monarch, Czar Nicholas II, who was unpopular. The nation had financial problems, and its military suffered losses in a 1905 war against Japan and in World War I. Nicholas's dissatisfied subjects revolted. Nicholas abdicated in 1917 and was executed, along with his wife and children, by the following year. A provisional government was in place until the Bolshevik Revolution overturned it, leading eventually to a Communist Party state that lasted approximately 70 years.

Another monarchial casualty of World War I was Germany. As it became clear Germany was going to be on the losing side of the war, the government prepared to battle the British navy anyway. German sailors mutinied, or revolted against their superiors. The locals in naval ports supported the sailors, which touched off the German Revolution against the imperial government. The revolution ended in the abdication of the monarchs in all of the German states, including the abdication of William II, also known as Kaiser Wilhelm II, emperor of Germany and king of Prussia, a state within the German empire. The monarchy ended, and a republic was established.

Coup d'État in China

While revolution ended several European monarchies early in the twentieth century, a coup d'état instigated the end of China's monarchy. A coup d'état is a revolution from within, which happens when a government or military leader overthrows the government.

That is what happened in China in 1911. At the time, a revolutionary movement was afoot to replace the Qing dynasty with a republic. Some of the revolutionaries were members of China's modernized New Army. One of the bombs built by the revolutionaries accidentally exploded, and when the police

SUCCESSION THREATS

When a sultan of the early Ottoman Empire died, his successor was supposed to be the most worthy person. That usually was a son but could be a brother, which sometimes led to a struggle. To avoid a succession dispute, when a sultan ascended the throne, he executed his brothers and his brothers' children. This removed all contenders for the throne except the sultan's offspring.

investigated, they found lists of revolutionaries' names. New Army soldiers who were on the list had to choose between being arrested—and probably executed—or revolting. They staged a coup in one province, which prompted the government of that province to flee. The revolutionaries then asked other provinces to join them. Fifteen agreed and seceded, and a provisional government was established. In 1912, the emperor, Puyi, abdicated, and the Republic of China was established with military leader Yuan Shikai as its first president. Later, mainland China became a communist state. Republican government continued on Taiwan, an island off China's coast. ⌘

HAWAIIAN MONARCHY ENDS

A revolution led by several businessmen ended the monarchy in Hawaii, once an independent state in the Pacific. The businessmen, who included American sugar and pineapple growers, wanted control of the island nation for their own profit. The group forced Hawaii's King Kalakaua to sign a constitution severely curtailing his powers and changing voting rules in a way that reduced native Hawaiians' say in their government. When the king's successor, his sister Queen Lili'uokalani, tried to create a new constitution, American troops moved in and forced her out of power. Hawaii was annexed as a territory of the United States in 1898.

8

Living in a Monarchy

A family jumps into an imported sedan and heads down a highway to a luxury shopping mall. The women of the group click along in their high heels as they browse offerings from high-end retailers such as Hermes, Gucci, and Rolex. After they make some purchases and lighten their wallets, they settle for an inexpensive meal at a fast-food franchise. This shopping excursion could have happened in London, Madrid, Toronto, or Tokyo, except all of the women in the mall are covered head-to-toe in black abayas and head scarves, and none of them drove to the mall

A Muslim woman wears a traditional burka while shopping.

themselves, since it is illegal for women to drive in their country. In this case, the shopping mall is in Riyadh, Saudi Arabia.

In some ways, life in one monarchy state bears similarities to others because designer clothes, fast-food chains, shopping malls, fancy cars, and paved highways can be found in cities around the globe. At the same time, nations with monarchies have many cultural differences that make life for those who live in one kingdom quite different from life in another.

ISLAM

The Prophet Muhammad founded the religion of Islam in the seventh century in what is now Saudi Arabia. Today, it has more than 1 billion followers worldwide. Followers of Islam, called Muslims, believe in one god, Allah. They also believe in angels and in the resurrection of humans after the end of the world. Devout Muslims give alms to the poor, pray five times each day, and make a pilgrimage to Mecca, the Prophet Muhammad's birthplace in Saudi Arabia.

Religion in Islamic Monarchies

Among all of the monarchies that call Islam their official religion—Bahrain, Brunei, Jordan, Kuwait, Oman, United Arab Emirates, Saudi Arabia, Qatar, Malaysia, and Morocco—at least some restrictions are placed upon religious freedom within their borders.

Malaysia prohibits the proselytizing of Muslims by non-Muslims, for example, and Oman prohibits religious gatherings in places other than government-approved houses of worship. In these countries, Islamic rules of conduct are followed by the general public, even non-Muslims. Dress codes that emphasize modesty, particularly for women, prevail. In some places, women may wear Western-style dress that covers the arms and knees, with a head scarf that covers the hair. In others, fabrics that completely cover a woman,

DATING IN AN ISLAMIC MONARCHY

Because of Islamic law in Saudi Arabia, dating is a challenge. Men must make judgments about a woman based on her eyes alone, since that is the only part of a woman visible in public. A 2003 account in *U.S. News & World Report* depicted young men and women exchanging glances in Riyadh's supermarkets, with women leaving their telephone numbers under the produce for the men. Using cell phones, a pair would arrange to have their first date in a Saudi restaurant, where they would go into the section designated for family and pretend to be married. "There, as their orders are taken, the veil comes off, and the man gets a first look at his date's face," wrote David E. Kaplan in the magazine piece.[1]

In Jordan, too, women risk damage to their reputation if seen with a male who is not a relative. Often they prefer to walk in the street rather than on sidewalks to avoid accidentally brushing up against male passersby. Young men and women, prohibited from meeting face-to-face without a chaperone, sometimes meet up in Internet cafés, where they can get to know each other by instant messaging.

even her face, are required in public. Nonetheless, all but Saudi Arabia allow their citizens to practice religions other than Islam.

In Saudi Arabia, the rules are particularly strict. No religion other than Islam can be practiced openly. In Saudi public schools, all children receive mandatory religious education in the Salafi tradition of Sunni Islam, which is the state's official tradition. In accordance with Islamic law, women cannot drive a car or ride a bicycle on public roads. Women are also prohibited from socializing publicly with men to whom they are not related. To conform to this prohibition, restaurants segregate, either by providing one section for men and another for families, or by not allowing women in at all. Saudi religious police enforce the rules.

In 2008, the religious police arrested a married American businesswoman for sitting with a male colleague in the family section of a Riyadh Starbucks. The woman, wearing the traditional abaya, had gone to the Starbucks with her male coworkers to use the store's wireless Internet connection because they had lost power in their office. "Some men came up to us with very long beards and white dresses," the woman told a British newspaper. "They asked 'Why are you here together?' I explained about the power being cut in our office. They got very angry and told me what I was doing was a great sin."[2] To her astonishment, the police seized her mobile phone, pushed her into a cab, and took her to a prison, where she was interrogated, strip-searched, and forced to sign a confession.

She was then taken before a judge, who declared she was sinful and was going to burn in hell. Her husband, a prominent businessman, was able to get her released after a day in prison.

In other Islamic monarchies, such as Jordan, religious rules are enforced mostly by family and society. For example, a woman who is suspected of immoral sexual behavior may be killed by her own family members for harming the family's honor. Women have also been killed for failing to accept an arranged marriage, or for seeking a divorce. While some in Jordan think such honor killings should be protected under the law,

HONOR KILLINGS

An honor killing is when a woman is killed by her family or by her community for what is thought to be immoral behavior. That behavior can include engaging in adultery, asking for a divorce, refusing an arranged marriage, or even being raped. While honor killings most often occur in Muslim countries, Islamic religion or law does not support the practice. Still, approximately two dozen women are victims of honor killings each year in Jordan, and those convicted of the crime have received as little as three months in jail. International human rights groups have asked Jordanian King Abdullah II to put a stop to the tradition and increase enforcement. Sentences recently have become somewhat harsher—in some cases up to ten years—but the perpetrators of honor killings still receive lighter sentences than other convicted murderers.

Jordanian courts insist they try and sentence honor crimes as they would other murders.

Some Islamic monarchies also monitor the consumption of alcoholic beverages and of pork. Because Muslims are not supposed to consume those items, those items are forbidden and unavailable in Saudi Arabia. In the United Arab Emirates, alcohol is available in some emirates, although not all. Also in Islamic countries, there are daily calls to prayer. Muslims are called from mosque towers or from loudspeakers in cities to pray five times each day—at sunrise, mid-morning, mid-afternoon, sunset, and at night. The Islamic Sabbath, when Muslims gather for prayer in the mosques, is on Friday. Women and men pray in separate sections in the mosques.

ROMAN CATHOLICISM

Roman Catholicism is a Christian religion. Like all Christians, Catholics worship one God and regard Jesus Christ as the Son of God, born on earth to save people from sin. The seat of the Roman Catholic Church is in Vatican City, in Rome, Italy. The Catholic Church is led by the Pope.

Religion in Other Monarchies

The Islamic monarchies are not the only ones with ties to religion. Christian and Buddhist monarchies allow more religious freedom than Islamic monarchies. Some European monarchies have ties to Protestant religions and, in fact, were instrumental in the creation of their state churches as they broke away from the Roman Catholic Church. In the United Kingdom, Queen Elizabeth II is the head of the Church of England, also called the Anglican Church, and is required to be a member of that faith. Members of the Church of England's hierarchy are seated in the House of Lords in Parliament. In Norway, King Harald V is the head of the Evangelical Lutheran Church, the state religion to which a vast majority of citizens belong. The king is required by law to be Lutheran. A government office administers the church, and the parliament votes on its budget. In Denmark, the Evangelical Lutheran Church of Denmark is the state church. Queen Margrethe and members of the royal house are required to be members,

PROTESTANT REFORMATION

In the sixteenth century, a German monk named Martin Luther broke from the Catholic Church to create the first Protestant church, known as the Lutheran Church. Luther questioned practices of the Roman Catholic Church, including its sale of indulgences, which exempted people from punishment for sins, and its leadership by the Pope. He also taught that belief in God, or faith, saves a person's soul and not simply doing good things. Today, Lutheranism is the state religion of Denmark and Norway. Since Luther's time, many more Protestant churches have been founded, including the Baptist Church, the Methodist Church, and the Anglican Church.

and a government office administers the organization. In addition, the government charges and collects a tax for the church and contributes toward clergy salaries and pensions.

A few European monarchies—all of them tiny—call Roman Catholicism their official religion. One is Vatican City, the city-state carved from Rome that is ruled by the Roman Catholic pope. The others are Monaco and Liechtenstein. Liechtenstein's government contributes to the Catholic Church but also contributes financially to other faiths. In Thailand and Cambodia, Theravada Buddhism is the official religion.

Political Rights

In addition to religious freedoms, most monarchies offer citizens political rights to some degree, although not the right to choose their monarchs. Living in most constitutional monarchies resembles living in a republic. Citizens elect politicians from among themselves to represent them in the national government and to make the laws. How many seats the citizens may fill is the variable. In the United Kingdom's bicameral parliament, politicians chosen by voters fill all of the seats in the House of Commons, and that chamber holds the lion's share of government power. From that chamber, the prime minister and most of the cabinet is chosen. The second chamber, called the House of Lords, is filled by heredity and by appointment.

Lesotho in Africa has a bicameral parliament as well. There, the lower house, which initiates legislation, is chosen by vote, and the upper house consists of 22 chiefs from the kingdom, as well as 11 members appointed by the political party that won the most seats in the lower house. Along similar lines is Cambodia, where the public chooses the members of the lower house but not of the upper house.

In countries with stronger monarchies, people have fewer political rights but still may participate in elections. In Oman, the sultan fills the upper house of the bicameral Council of Oman by appointments, but in the lower house members are elected by popular vote. Both houses have only advisory powers, however, and political parties are prohibited. Jordan allows political parties and fills its lower parliamentary chamber through elections. However, the king can dissolve parliament and did so in November 2009

GRADUAL CHANGE IN OMAN

Oman has a history of an absolute monarchy, in which the sultan is both the head of government and head of state. In 1991, Sultan Qaboos held the first election for members of the Consultative Assembly, the lower house of the Council of Oman, to increase public participation in government. At first, a limited number of citizens were eligible to vote to fill the 83 seats. Then, on October 4, 2003, the sultan instituted universal suffrage for citizens over age 21. However, the sultan retains the power to overturn the election results. The Consultative Assembly serves in an advisory capacity and has no power to pass legislation.

because he contended the body did not move fast enough on his program of economic reform. New elections were scheduled for November 2010. In Saudi Arabia, political parties are not allowed, and speaking against the government is prohibited. Peaceful critics of the government can be arrested and imprisoned without trial.

Taxes and Public Services

As political and religious rights vary from monarchy to monarchy, so do the public services provided by the government. For example, Brunei, which has a lucrative oil and natural gas business, charges no personal income tax and no sales tax while offering its citizens free health care. The government also subsidizes food, fuel, and housing costs.

Saudi Arabia, which also profits from petroleum, charges its citizens no personal income tax, although it charges a religious tax called *Zakat* that is used to help the poor and needy. Saudi Arabia also offers its citizens free health care. Saudi Arabia's neighboring monarchies, Kuwait, Oman, Qatar, and the United Arab Emirates, do not charge personal income tax, either, while providing health care free of charge to their citizens. Bahrain became the first of the Gulf monarchies to tax income. That kingdom offers mostly free but also some subsidized health care.

Income tax is common in the world's European monarchies, although Monaco is an exception. Most European monarchies provide free health care, funded by revenue from high income and sales taxes. In the United Kingdom, some citizens pay as much as half of their income in taxes. Health care in Spain is also financed through taxes. The more money a person makes, the higher percentage of income tax that person owes. The wealthiest people in Spain must pay close to half of their income in taxes. ⌘

9

Monarchies and International Relations

In June 2010, Saudi Arabia's King Abdullah met with US President Barack Obama at the White House. There, the king and the president discussed the war in Afghanistan between the United States and the Taliban, an extremist Islamic group. They also discussed reported attempts by the Islamic Republic of Iran to develop its nuclear weapons capacity, the ongoing conflict between Israel and the Palestinians, and the economy. "I always value his

---

US President Barack Obama met with Saudi Arabia's King Abdullah on June 29, 2010.

majesty's wisdom and insights," President Obama said following his private meeting with the king.[1]

King Abdullah recalled how the relationship between Saudi Arabia and the United States began decades ago following a meeting between the late US president Franklin Roosevelt and the late Saudi king Abdul Aziz Al Saud. "Over the past seven decades, the relationship has grown stronger and broader and deeper. . . . I hope that you will be able to continue to work with us on improving this relationship for many more years," King Abdullah told President Obama.[2]

The meeting between President Obama and King Abdullah is an example of direct diplomacy, a vital part of any monarch's job. But with so many countries and even more issues with international effects, heads of government do not have the time to personally negotiate every issue. The responsibility is delegated to others in the government, such as the minister for foreign affairs, a cabinet-level position in parliamentary monarchies. The minister works with the head of government to formulate foreign policy. Those ministers head bureaucracies devoted to support-ing diplomacy and their governments' foreign policy aims. Heads of government also appoint ambassadors, who are sent to represent their government's interests in other countries.

Nominal constitutional monarchs are not directly involved in their nations' foreign policies. They have no power to negotiate treaties or to authorize military alliances or actions.

Nonetheless, they often have a role in for-eign relations. They make international visits as representatives of their nations. Queen Elizabeth II, known for her extensive world travel, made a well-received and favorably publicized trip to the United States and Canada during the summer of 2010. Nominal monarchs also act as hosts to heads of state and dignitaries visiting from other lands.

International Organizations

International organizations provide another way for governments to relate to one another. Among the best known is the United Nations (UN), an organization that counts 192 of the world's nations as members. That includes 43 of the world's 44 monarchies—the exception being the Holy See, or Vatican City. Established in 1945 at the conclusion of World War II, the United Nations lists as its objectives the maintenance of international peace and security, the development of friendly relations among nations, and the promotion of social progress, better living standards, and human rights. Nations participate in this process

KING ABDULLAH'S PRAYER

During the press conference following King Abdullah meeting with President Obama in June 2010, the king uttered a prayer for the American media, which does not operate freely in his country.

"May God spare us from all of the bad things they can do to us," the king said. There was some chuckling in the room. Then he said, "And may God bless us with all the positive things they can do for us and for humanity." President Obama responded, "Well, that is an excellent prayer. Thank you."[3]

by sending representatives to the UN, which has headquarters in New York City and offices worldwide.

Sometimes the UN's work involves criticizing the actions of members. In April 2010, UN High Commissioner for Human Rights Navi Pillay, expressed concern about the treatment of migrant workers in the six monarchies in the Persian Gulf. During a visit to Saudi Arabia, Pillay said reports "consistently cite ongoing practices

INTERNATIONAL ORGANIZATIONS

Dozens of international organizations exist for countries to work together toward mutual interests. The Commonwealth of Nations, headed by Queen Elizabeth II, is an association of 54 cooperating nations including the 16 Commonwealth realms. The Organization for Economic Cooperation and Development is an association of 31 countries that are committed to democracy and a market economy. Twelve monarchies are members. The International Energy Agency acts as an energy policy adviser for its 28 member countries. More than 150 nations are members of the World Trade Organization, within which agreements are made concerning how international commerce will be conducted, with the objective of trade happening as freely as possible. Almost all of the monarchies are members, with a few—Andorra, Bhutan, and Holy See (Vatican City)—listed as observers that may one day become members. The North Atlantic Treaty Organization (NATO) includes 28 countries, all of which agreed if one of its members were attacked militarily, it would be viewed as an attack on all. NATO members work together on defense, military, and security issues, and to promote democratic values. Working together on joint defense in the Middle East is the Gulf Cooperation Council, consisting of the six Persian Gulf monarchies.

of unlawful confiscation of passports, withholding of wages, and exploitation by unscrupulous recruitment agencies and employers."[4] She asked countries to adopt updated labor laws that protect migrant workers. In July 2010, the Gulf monarchies formed a human rights panel to ensure the protection of migrant workers and to help guard against other human rights abuses.

The UN can use trade embargoes and military action to penalize governments it judges to be a threat to world peace and security. The UN Security Council, the organization within the United Nations that copes with threats to international peace and security, includes one monarchy—the United Kingdom—among the five nations that are permanent members. In 2010, Japan was among ten non-permanent members that sit on the Security Council for two-year terms following election by the UN General Assembly.

One of the most prominent international government organizations is the European Union (EU), which consists of 27 nations. The EU behaves a bit like a country of its own because each member has given up sovereignty in some areas to the organization. For example, some of the member nations gave up the right to have their own currency in favor of a common European currency called the euro. In another measure, the group established a carbon emissions trading system in 2005 as a way to reduce the amount of carbon gases entering the atmosphere.

Sometimes international organizations work together. For instance, in July 2010 the EU and the Gulf Cooperation Council, which consists of the six monarchies in the Persian Gulf, announced plans to conduct annual meetings to improve trade between the two regional blocks. Already the groups have met twice, most recently in Brussels, Belgium, to discuss the global economic crisis, with apparent satisfactory results.

Peter Bekx, director for international economic and financial affairs at the European Commission, stated, "We exchanged views on a number of very important issues like how to exit from the economic crisis, and monetary and regional integration. I think we both can learn from each other's experience."[5]

Trade

Additionally, nations relate through trade. One of the primary commodities traded among monarchy states is petroleum, a resource largely responsible for the wealth of the six

IRAN'S NUCLEAR PROGRAM

In 2010, the UN Security Council increased sanctions against Iran after learning that country was developing a nuclear program, which some believed involved nuclear weapons. The United Kingdom and Japan were among the nations voting in favor of the sanctions, which included expanding an embargo on arms to Iran and tightening restrictions on shipping and financial enterprises related to Iran's nuclear activity. Iran's UN representative said his country "would not bow to such pressures" and asserted "his country's right to use nuclear technology for peaceful purposes."[6]

monarchies in the Persian Gulf—Bahrain, Kuwait, Oman, Qatar, Saudi Arabia, and the United Arab Emirates—as well as Brunei, a small nation on the South China Sea. The world depends upon petroleum as an energy source for automobiles, trucks, airplanes, ships, and industrial processes, and the Arab nations hold huge supplies of it. Saudi Arabia alone holds an estimated 20 percent of the world's oil reserves.[7]

Many of the relationships forged between the Arab petroleum states and other nations in the world are connected to the supply of petroleum. The Gulf economies depend largely on the business of petroleum, of which they are net exporters, and other nations in the world, particularly the United States, are big oil consumers and depend on imported oil from Saudi Arabia and from other oil exporters to keep their industrialized economies running. Another big oil producer is Canada, from which the United States buys more petroleum than from any other country. The two countries, which share a very long border in North America, have a good relationship. One of the benefits Canada reaps from that is that the United States buys almost 80 percent of what Canada exports each year, the CIA reported.[8]

Monarchies, whether big or small, rich or poor, trade a variety of goods and services. Inside the EU, the member nations have a close economic relationship, with a common currency (except for Denmark, Sweden, and the United Kingdom) and with no trade barriers such as tariffs. Many European countries, such as Belgium, export manufactured goods but rely upon the import of raw materials from other countries to make them. In Asia, Bhutan depends on India for trade and also for financial assistance. Bhutan's largely undeveloped economy is based on agriculture and forestry, although its hydropower business is boosting its growth. Cambodia's garment industry employs about 5 percent of the nation's workforce and is responsible for about 70 percent of its exports to other countries.[9] Jordan, a small economy in the Middle East, does not have enough of its own water, oil, or other natural resources and therefore relies on supplies of those resources from other countries. Lesotho in Africa relies on trading with neighboring South Africa but also counts the United States as an important trade partner for its clothing exports.

The list of interdependency goes on. No nation, monarchy or not, operates solely on its own. All nations rely on others for markets for

MONARCHS AS DIPLOMATS

Yale historian Frank Prochaska wrote in his book *The Eagle and the Crown: Americans and the British Monarchy* about the influence British monarchs can have over leaders of foreign countries because of their exalted status. Using diplomacy, members of the British royalty can subtly promote the interests of their homeland and improve international relations. "The King and Queen were not decisive pieces on the international chess board, but they were influential pawns."[10]

their goods and for raw materials and products their countries do not have. They also work with others to come to agreements on how business will be done and on how peace will be kept so that business can continue. ⌘

10

Monarchies, Media, and Celebrity

In 1980, a journalist who covered the British royal family for a London newspaper was watching Charles, Prince of Wales, outside his mother's castle in Scotland. Suddenly, he spotted light reflecting from behind a tree. The prince was not alone; a woman was hiding behind the tree, holding up a makeup mirror to glimpse the journalist. "On her very first public sighting . . . Lady Diana Spencer was craftily watching the press as they craftily watched her," biographer

LA VANGUARDIA

Trágico final de lady Di

La dramática muerte de Diana levanta una gran controversia sobre el acoso de los "paparazzi"

el Periódico

LADY DI NO SUPERÓ LAS GRAVES HERIDAS DEL ACCIDENTE

Diana, nace un mito

Carlos de Inglaterra recibió en París el féretro de su ex esposa que reposa en una capilla privada

Estupor y consternación en todo el mundo por la inesperada muerte de la princesa

elPeriódico

El Barça toma el mando de la Liga el primer día

El Espanyol arranca tres puntos en Bilbao

PAÍS

...des de todo el mundo se ... por la muerte de Diana

DEPORTES

El Barcelona, primer líder de la Liga

EL ● MUNDO

Su muerte conmociona al mundo

La familia Spencer culpa a la prensa y encabeza un alud de críticas contra los excesos de los 'paparazzi'

Al chófer del Ritz se le doblaba el coche a más de 150 Km/h.

Ofrecen la fotografía del cadáver por un millón de dólares

Muere una princesa, ha nacido un mito

Su hijo merece el mejor Colegio.

COLEGIO MONT...

DIARIO

BOICOT DE TELEFÓNICA AL FÚTBOL E...

EDICIÓN ...

TRISTE DIANA

● Conmoción mundial por la muerte de 'Lady Di'...
● La detención de los siete 'paparazzi' dispara la polémica ...

Robert Lacey wrote.[1] Soon, a front-page newspaper headline declared Charles to be in love.

Press coverage of Charles and Diana ramped up during their courtship and, according to Lacey, pressure from the press helped instigate a marriage proposal. The pair married in July 1981. In the subsequent 16 years, Diana became one of the most photographed women in the world, a near-constant presence in newspapers and on magazine covers. But her marriage was not to last. The press, sometimes with the consent of the parties, chronicled the marriage's devolution. Diana contributed behind the scenes to a journalist's 1992 biography of her. In the book, Charles and the royal family were painted in an unflattering light. Diana and Charles separated that year. Later, Charles collaborated on a television documentary and a book about himself in which he admitted his infidelity with Camilla Parker-Bowles. Diana participated in her own television documentary, in which she portrayed herself as a wife victimized by her husband's infidelity, although she discussed a love affair of her own.

SELLING NEWSPAPERS

Roy Greensdale of the British newspaper the *Guardian* said royalty news sells newspapers because the public wants it: "This is a celebrity-driven age in which the public cannibalizes its idols and the royal family are the ultimate celebrities."[2]

After the 1996 divorce, the press continued to follow Diana. They covered her philanthropic endeavors, such as her activism on behalf of land mine victims and people with AIDS, as well as her romantic pursuits. It was the latter for which the press followed her to Paris in August 1997, when she was on holiday with a new boyfriend, Dodi al-Fayed. Paparazzi followed Diana's car at high speeds into a Paris tunnel, when the Mercedes crashed, killing Diana, al-Fayed, and the driver of the car, Henri Paul. Later it was revealed that the driver had been intoxicated. But Diana's brother, Charles Spencer, placed the blame on the press when he eulogized his sister at her funeral.

Monarchs as Celebrities

Royals have always been in the news because of their positions of power.

PRINCES HARRY AND WILLIAM

The sons of Princess Diana and Prince Charles often appear in gossip columns for their romances. In November 2010, the media went all out covering the news that Prince William, heir to the throne after his father, had proposed marriage to his longtime girlfriend, Kate Middleton. Articles about the engagement covered everything from speculation about the royal wedding to comparisons with the romance of William's parents.

Gossip columns have noted Prince Harry's romances as well as his active nightlife. Prince Harry also generated negative press when he wore an armband bearing a swastika to a friend's party in 2005 and when he made racial comments in 2009.

*Prince William and
Kate Middleton, 2008*

But in the past century, the Western media has focused as much on royals' personal lives as on their political roles. Coverage also has focused more on the younger royals—the children of the reigning monarchs, who had fewer official responsibilities but were attractive, rich, and had active social and romantic lives. At the same time, royal families have courted the press, hoping to boost their public image and thus preserve their status. For example, the British royal family agreed to be a subject of a documentary in the 1960s so their citizens would see their day-to-day lives, an attempt at making the royals seem more normal and accessible to common people.

It showed, among other things, Prince Philip barbecuing at Balmoral Castle. *Royal Family* was seen by more than 200 million people and was considered a wild success, but the queen turned down requests to show it again. "It was soon realized . . . that showing the royals to be mere mortals was a double-edged sword," Lacey wrote.[3]

Royals have an exalted status in society, and when they are portrayed in the media as "just like everyone else," it calls that status into question. "The revelation of royal family secrets tends to bring the monarchy into disrepute," wrote Roy Greenslade in the *Guardian*. "By training the spotlight on them, they undermine the notion of the family's supposedly special place at the apex of society."[4]

IMAGE CONTROL IN JAPAN

In Japan, the Imperial Household Agency carefully controls what is written about the imperial family. In April of 2005, Irish journalist David McNeill was supposed to be allowed to ask the emperor two questions during a televised press conference before the imperial couple's trip to Ireland. McNeill wanted to ask the emperor his opinion on whether the national anthem should be required at school ceremonies, and he submitted his questions weeks in advance for approval. Nonetheless, agency officials ushered out television cameras covering the event just as McNeill rose to speak, out of fear that as a foreigner he would say something to embarrass the emperor. Most journalists' questions during the conference concerned uncontroversial matters such as the emperor's health.

In the 1950s and 1960s, the press chronicled the active love life and party life of Princess Margaret, Queen Elizabeth II's younger sister. Press photographers caught her in scandalous romances. After actress Grace Kelly married Prince Rainier of Monaco, media coverage focused on the romances of their children, particularly daughters Caroline and Stephanie. The press also kept tabs on Princess Stephanie's forays into fashion design and pop singing. Then, in the 1980s and 1990s came the saturation coverage of Princess Diana, although some room was left for reporting on the dissolution of Prince Andrew's marriage. That came after the press caught his wife, Sarah, with other men.

"What is the monarchy now, if not a ceaseless media roadshow, selling nothing but itself? How can the royal family exist in the public consciousness, if not through the flashbulbs and omnipresent cameras?" asked Johann Hari in the *New Statesman*.[5]

Controlling the Media

Because public image is so important, monarchies do their best to control what is reported about them. Absolute monarchs often control public media as a way to limit any opposition's ability to organize and get its message out. The press also is used to indoctrinate citizens with a positive view of the government. Success in that regard reduces opposition. Among such states is Saudi Arabia, which is largely intolerant of criticism by the press or anyone else of the royal family, of the government, or of the state religion, Islam.

In Saudi Arabia, no separation of church and state exists. The state controls all television broadcasting and newspapers by royal decree. Newspapers within the country tend to self-censor regarding sensitive subjects because Saudi Arabia's Basic Law, the nation's constitution, places broad restrictions on media and publications, including prohibitions from printing anything that fosters division, harms the state's public relations, or detracts from human dignity. Newspapers from outside the country are subject to censorship, and website access is blocked by the government if content is determined to be offensive. The government controls foreign media outlets by requiring licensing and by delaying or preventing the distribution of foreign print material. Journalists occasionally face government harassment. In one example, a prince called a sports channel during a live broadcast after the national soccer team lost a game. He threatened the commentator, who had made negative remarks about the team and about the management of the soccer federation. The soccer federation is reportedly affiliated with the royal family.

Saudi Arabia is not the only monarchy with a tightly controlled press. Jordan has a constitution with press protections, but journalists still face the threat of detention, imprisonment, and steep fines under the press and publications law for defamation. These threats have led the press to censor itself. The government of Jordan has also provided special treatment to favored journalists, such as scholarships for relatives, as a means of control. Brunei's newspapers also have practiced self-censorship. There, the Sedition Act makes it illegal to challenge the authority of the sultan and the royal family or to challenge the nation's monarchy concept. Members of the press who break the rules can be fined, imprisoned, or prohibited from working in the field.

Fear of reprisal is not limited to the strong monarchies in the Persian Gulf region, however. In Swaziland in Africa, journalists also practice self-censorship because of government threats. One example the State Department cited was that of freelance journalist and *Times of*

LÈSE MAJESTÉ LAWS

In Thailand, where King Bhumibol Adulyadej is a revered figure, it is against the law to insult or defame the monarchy under a set of laws called *lèse majesté.* Those charged with the offense face up to 15 years in jail. Anyone can charge anyone else with the crime, and the police are obliged to investigate. Because of that, critics say, the law is used politically, with opponents charging each other with the offense. For example, in June 2010, the Puea Thai Party accused Thailand's foreign minister Kasit Piromya with violating *lèse majesté* because of remarks he made in April 2010

advocating reform of the monarchy. The government also has cited the laws as its reason for shutting down more than 40,000 Web sites.

For his part, in June 2010 the king, who was hospitalized, pardoned a man who had been sentenced to ten years imprisonment for doctoring images of the royal family before posting them on the web. One news report said the king often pardons those who are convicted. The king has said: "Actually, I must also be criticized. I am not afraid if the criticism concerns what I do wrong, because then I know."[6]

Swaziland columnist Vusi Sibisi. After Sibisi wrote articles that were critical of the government and of the monarchy, a warrant was issued for his arrest. Sibisi stopped writing. In Thailand, the press is permitted to criticize the government, but not the king or queen. Laws called *lèse majesté* strictly forbid such criticism. Even foreign tourists have been arrested and jailed for speaking against King Bhumibol. The Thai government curtailed press freedoms during a period of civil unrest in 2009. Harassment of and violence against journalists was reported, although sometimes that came at the hands of political activists and not the government. The Thai government tolerates press criticism, the state department reported, unless it is about the monarchy.

In Cambodia, the constitution declares the king inviolable, secure from attack or violation. A government directive prohibits publishers and editors from publishing stories that insult government leaders or institutions. In Morocco, criticism of Islam and the monarchy is illegal. Weekly newsmagazines have been seized because they printed opinions about the king's first decade in power. In addition, some reporters were imprisoned and fined for reporting false information about the king's health. ⌘

Downsides to Modern Monarchies

Wearing a cream-colored designer satin gown with an off-the-shoulder neckline, Crown Princess Victoria of Sweden, heiress to the Swedish throne, married Daniel Westling, her former personal trainer, in a June 19, 2010, ceremony at Stockholm's Storkyrkan cathedral. Approximately 1,200 people attended the wedding and reception, including royalty from Norway, Denmark, Netherlands, Luxembourg, Spain, Jordan, England, Belgium, and Monaco.

Crown Princess Victoria of Sweden and her fiancé Daniel Westling attend a government reception on June 18, 2010, as part of their wedding celebration.

With any big party comes a big bill, and the Swedish royal wedding was no exception. The wedding cost 20 million Swedish kronor, approximately $2.7 million in US currency.[1] King Carl XVI Gustaf paid half, while Swedish taxpayers paid the other half. The government also spent 77 million kronor, or $10.2 million, on the attendant two-week Love Stockholm festival, which featured celebrations and performances of the arts.[2]

WEALTHY MONARCHS

Governments spend money on their monarchs even though some monarchs are independently wealthy. In 2009, *Forbes* magazine listed Queen Elizabeth II's personal fortune at $450 million and that of Queen Beatrix of the Netherlands at $200 million. *Forbes* noted that Swaziland King Mswati III was worth $100 million. Japan's emperor did not make Forbes's Top 15 list of the world's wealthy monarchs, nor did the monarchs of Norway, Belgium, Denmark, Spain, Luxembourg, or Sweden. Two other European monarchs did make the list: Prince Hans-Adam II of Liechtenstein, worth $3.5 billion, and Prince Albert II of Monaco, worth $1 billion. The world's richest royal, according to Forbes, was King Bhumibol of Thailand, worth $30 billion. Most of the others on the list are kings, sultans, and sheikhs who are rulers in oil-rich Arab states.[3]

Monarchies Can Be Costly

The main reason people are opposed to monarchies is the high cost of maintaining them. The cost to the United Kingdom of supporting the British royal family in the 2009–2010 fiscal year was £38.2 million, or $60 million, according to a report in England's *Daily Telegraph*.[4] This figure includes costs for entertaining, travel expenses, salaries for more than 1,000 staff members, and the maintenance of buildings such as Buckingham Palace, which is owned by the United Kingdom and is the queen's London address. However, the figure does not include security costs, which are kept secret. Some critics place the cost of the British monarchy at about £180 million ($271 million), when security expenses and the cost of having the Royal Armed Forces participate in royal events are added in.[5]

Herman Matthijs, a professor at the Free University of Brussels, released findings that the British monarchy was the most expensive in Europe. In 2009, Matthijs reported, the British monarchy cost £41.5 million, or $65.7 million.[6] During the same year, the Dutch monarchy cost £33.8 million, or $53.6 million, the Norwegian monarchy cost £23.9 million, or $37.9 million, and the Belgian monarchy cost £11.7 million, or $18.5 million.[7] The annual government expenditure on the monarchy in Denmark in 2009 was almost 90 million Danish kroner ($15.2 million), according to a Danish government report.[8] That was approximately the same as what was spent on the Swedish monarchy, according to Matthijs's report. The amount Britain spent on its monarchy was six times what Spain and Luxembourg spent on theirs.

Not included in Matthijs's study was Japan, which some reports contended was much more expensive than the British monarchy. A 1998 report published by the *Atlantic* indicated the Japanese monarchy cost the government $200 million that year.[9] That included the salaries of 1,150 imperial employees and 970 palace police officers. The emperor earned a fraction of that: a $2.4 million tax-free stipend from which he paid daily living expenses for his family and for research assistants for his study of Gobi fish. A 2005 report by journalist David McNeill placed the cost of the Japanese monarchy at about $260 million but pointed out that the emperor had approximately $56,000 a year to spend on himself.[10]

In Swaziland, the 2010 budget set aside $30 million for royal compensation, although the king's income may exceed that, according to the *New York Times*.[11] King Mswati III's spending has been unpopular in his poverty-stricken country, where he has

ROYALTY IN RECESSION

Press reports in the summer of 2010 noted Queen Elizabeth II and heir to the throne Prince Charles were cutting expenses in light of the global economic recession. That did not satisfy some opponents of the monarchy. "When public spending is being slashed across the board, it's time to cut his [Prince Charles's] bill to the taxpayer to zero," said Graham Smith, campaign manager of Republic, an antimonarchist group.[12]

given each of his 13 wives a palace, a BMW, and a group of attendants. Mswati's spending prompted thousands of citizens to protest, the *New York Times* reported in 2008.

Monarchs Are Born, Not Elected

While expense is one argument used against keeping a monarchy government, another is that most citizens have no say over who sits on the throne. Monarchs usually are born into royal families and ascend the throne following rules of succession that have to do with when one is born, not with whether the sovereign is able to perform the responsibilities well or has the confidence of the people over whom he or she will reign.

Some opponents of monarchies argue that an elected president could perform the same role of national symbol ascribed to royals, but with one difference: voters could toss out a president who was not performing as expected, while royals serve for life. Lewis Holden, chair of the Republican Movement of Aotearoa New Zealand, wrote:

> *Having a say in who is head of state, even if the job is ceremonial, is better than having no say. If our elected head of state is found to be inadequate, we can elect a new one. Sure, it's not perfect, but it's certainly better than a genetic lottery. And more importantly, electing our head of state emphasizes where power comes from—the people.*[13]

Inappropriate Behavior

Monarchs do not always perform the way the citizens expect. Recently, England's Prince Charles came under fire for his seemingly political behavior in a nation where the royals are expected to behave apolitically. In one instance, Prince Charles wrote a letter to the developer of a London property expressing displeasure over the design of the project. His intervention led the development company to withdraw the plan. Charles's private secretary said the letter expressed and gave exposure to the views of unhappy local residents. However, a constitutional expert argued the prince could not do such things once he becomes king. "The constitution is silent on the role and responsibilities of the deputy head of state. But I would think all constitutional experts would agree that he can't behave like this when he is sovereign because the sovereign has to be impeccably neutral," said Robert Hazell, director of the constitutional unit at University College London.[14]

Several members of the British royal family have been involved in scandals, including Sarah Ferguson, the Duchess of

"Monarchy is incompatible with democracy. According to the elitist values of the monarchical system, the most stupid, immoral royal is more fit to be head of state than the wisest, most ethical commoner. Monarchs get the job for life, no matter how appallingly they behave."[15]

—*Peter Tatchell, British human rights activist*

York and former wife of Prince Charles's younger brother Andrew. Photographers caught the duchess with another man while she was still married to Andrew in 1992. More recently, in 2010, she was caught trying to sell reporters access to Prince Andrew. Sophie, Duchess of Wessex, was caught on tape gossiping about the royal family and government. Sophie is married to Prince Edward, the youngest brother of Prince Charles. Remarked author and commentator Chalmers Johnson, "What are royal families anywhere good for these days? Mainly laughs."[16]

The British royals are not the only royals whose behavior has caused scandal. Princess Stephanie of Monaco became known for her wild lifestyle, which included a succession of boyfriends, children born outside marriage, and two divorces, once because her husband was caught in photographs with another woman. When Prince Albert II, the brother of Stephanie and Caroline, became engaged in 2010, news stories noted he had fathered two children out of wedlock with two different women.

In Norway, Prince Haakon was criticized for his relationship with Mette-Marit Tjessem Hoiby, who had a child with a man convicted of drug offenses. The prince's decision to live with her before they were married in 2001 brought some complaints from the public and from the Lutheran Church. In the Netherlands, Prince Johan Friso gave up his spot in the line of succession when he married Mabel Wisse Smit without the permission of Parliament, as required by Dutch law. That decision came after Wisse Smit admitted she had given incorrect information to the government about her prior relationship with a criminal.

THOMAS PAINE

In his 1776 pamphlet *Common Sense*, English immigrant Thomas Paine argued the American colonies should separate from England. One of his arguments to do so was that a monarchy, which was England's form of government, separated mankind, in which all were supposed to be equal, into unequal categories: king and subjects. Paine also argued against the idea of succession:

> *For all men being originally equals, no one by birth could have a right to set up his own family in perpetual preference to all others for ever, and tho' himself might deserve some decent degree of honours of his contemporaries, yet his descendants might be far too unworthy to inherit them.*[17]

Monarchs Are Tied to Social Class System

Unconventional behavior aside, some opponents say monarchies should be abolished for philosophical reasons. Specifically, they say the monarchy is tied to an outdated social class system that dictated some people were better than others and deserved more privileges simply because they were born into upper-class, noble, or royal families. Monarchy reinforces class distinctions by giving one family special prominence, power, wealth, and social standing for no reason other than heredity. "Such gross inequality which permits individuals who have personally achieved little and done nothing substantive for the benefits they receive to be elevated above all others is surely intolerable to any thinking person," wrote columnist Claire Rayner in the *Guardian*, a British newspaper.[18] The Socialist Party in the United Kingdom makes the same argument on its Web site: that the monarchy is the living embodiment of a hierarchical society. Some opponents find monarchies to be elitist and argue only common people should have a role in government.

British politician Roy Hattersley summed up arguments against the monarchy form of government this way:

> The monarchy has three detrimental effects on society: it epitomizes and encourages the idea of a social hierarchy; it is based on the belief that blood and birth, rather than personal merit, are enough to justify respect or even admiration; it encourages nostalgia for the past, in which it is firmly rooted, rather than hope for the future. It is also very expensive.[19] ⌘

Positive Attributes of Modern Monarchies

Monarchies have been around since antiquity and continue to prosper today. It stands to reason, then, that there must be something good about them, something that gives staying power to a system of government that is headed by a person who likely inherited his or her position from someone else in the family. It is a particularly interesting phenomenon in the constitutional monarchies of parliamentary democracies, where the king or queen or

Prime Minister Winston Churchill and Queen Elizabeth II, 1955

emperor has nominal power. If the elected government does the governing, why have a monarch?

One reason is that monarchs are a constant in constantly changing political landscapes. Political parties acquire and lose power, parliaments open and dissolve, governments form and end, politicians are elected, reelected, or not. Regardless, the king, queen, sultan or emperor remains on the throne, and the royal family remains in place, providing a link for its people to a common past. It is a point the British royal family makes on its official Web site: "A constitutional monarchy . . . provides stability, continuity and a national focus, as the Head of State remains the same even as governments change."[1] The royal family's Web site notes Queen Elizabeth II, who ascended the throne in 1952, has reigned during the administrations of 12 different prime ministers, beginning with Winston Churchill just after World War II. In fact, as of 2010, Elizabeth had reigned 12 years longer than British Prime Minister David Cameron had been alive.

> "For the Queen they still have great affections and respect, which is not surprising since of all our great institutions, the monarchy is the only one which actually works. Unlike aristocracy, which divided the nation, monarchy holds it together."[2]
>
> —*Peregrine Worsthorne, British journalist*

The Monarch as Unifier

Furthermore, as members of the British royal family have mentioned, monarchs can help unify a nation. Different peoples from different ethnic backgrounds may populate a nation, but they all share one sovereign. Such is the case in Spain and Belgium. In Spain, regions called autonomous communities have their own language and cultures. Among them is Basque Country, where a secessionist movement is active. Because King Juan Carlos I, as Spain's king, is the monarch for all of Spain's different regions, he could be a factor in keeping the country together, some say. "As the autonomous regions become ever more powerful and Spain becomes a quasi-federalist nation, the King can serve as a unifying force," wrote Tom Burns Marañon, author of *Conversations on the King*. "Cohesion depends on the personality of the King. He needs to be very sensitive to the differences."[3]

In Belgium, linguistic disputes exist in a nation where Dutch, or Flemish, is spoken in the north, and French is spoken in the south. Another region is home to German speakers. Political disagreement also exists over government aid going to the less affluent, French-speaking region. In Belgium as in Spain, there is talk of secession. A separatist party from the Flemish-speaking Flanders region won the most seats in parliament in the June 2010 elections. No party had a majority, and it was King Albert II's responsibility to negotiate the formation of a coalition government. In Belgium and Spain, "There is an internal problem of autonomy," wrote Francis

Delpérée, a constitutional law expert at Belgium's University of Louvain. "Like Juan Carlos in Spain, King Albert II represents a symbol of unity in a much-divided country."[4]

In other European kingdoms, Sweden's Carl XVI Gustaf is noted for calling the integration of immigrants a priority, while the Netherlands' Queen Beatrix has called for ethnic tolerance. In her December 2007 Christmas speech, Queen Beatrix urged Dutch citizens to be more tolerant, saying, "Our democratic tradition comprises more than only the acceptance of the power of the majority; it is also about respect for minorities."[5]

Queen Elizabeth II is seen as a unifier as well, reigning over not just the United Kingdom, which consists of the four countries of England, Scotland, Wales, and Northern Ireland, but also over the 15 other Commonwealth realms. The realms are quite varied and include a host of Caribbean

QUEEN BEATRIX

In the Netherlands, Queen Beatrix exercises more authority than some of her fellow constitutional monarchs in Europe. She is both head of state and a member of the government, where she has a hand in legislation. She is president of the Council of State, the government's main advisory body. Beatrix ascended the throne in 1980 at age 42 when her mother abdicated in her favor. Some have speculated Beatrix will soon do the same to hand power to her son, Crown Prince Willem-Alexander, who is in his forties.

Queen Beatrix of the Netherlands is pictured on a stamp.

islands, Canada in North America, and Australia in the Southern Hemisphere. But they all share a common monarch, a fact that binds them. "If we abolished [the monarchy], we would remove those ties,"[6] noted Jessica Walker, a British citizen who moved from England to New Zealand. Additionally, Elizabeth II is the head of the Commonwealth of Nations, a voluntary association of 54 countries that work together toward shared goals of democracy and development. It is another place where Elizabeth II's presence can be seen as a unifier.

The Monarch as a Neutral Leader

In New Zealand, the monarchist group Monarchy New Zealand contends that having a hereditary head of state ensures that at least one person in the government is not beholden to special interests:

> Hereditary appointment is a neutral way to select a head of state. It ensures that he or she will be above partisan politics and that the head of state will have the best interest of the whole nation at heart, not just the interests of those who elected or appointed him or her. No elected official could ever claim to represent an entire nation because he or she owes their position to only those who voted in her favor.[7]

The perceived neutrality that comes from not being subject to political election also can be an asset as a monarch acts as a diplomat and ambassador to other nations. An example was the July 6, 2010, visit of Queen Elizabeth II to New York City in the United States. During the visit, the queen placed a wreath of flowers at the site of the September 11, 2001, terrorist attack on the World Trade Center, where almost 3,000 people died, and officially opened the British Garden of Remembrance, which honors the 67 Britons killed in the terrorist attacks. As queen of the Commonwealth realms and as head of the Commonwealth of Nations, she also spoke to the UN, praising the organization for its work promoting peace, fighting poverty, and protecting human rights. The queen did or said nothing controversial or political and was welcomed warmly during her visit, according to press reports, which featured her in a positive light.

Being a neutral head of state unaffiliated with any political party can help the monarch resolve disputes in government. In 1981, military conspirators held 350 people hostage in Spain's parliament in an attempted coup d'état. King Juan Carlos spent the night calling military commanders to secure their loyalty and made a television address asking the citizens to remain

MONARCHISTS

Many people feel strongly about the continuation of their countries' monarchical governments. Supporters of monarchies are called monarchists. Dozens of organizations exist to promote the advantages of monarchies and work to keep the world's monarchies alive. The International Monarchy League, for example, was created following World War II to help preserve the European monarchies. The organization continues to promote monarchies as a stable, nonpartisan, and beneficial form of government.

calm. The coup failed. An article in the magazine *Canada and the World Backgrounder* argued:

> Anybody looking for a reason to hold on to a monarchy in this modern age found it right there. King Juan Carlos I stared down a group of violent men bent on destroying a democracy. Without his timely and effective action, the country might have sunk into another harsh dictatorship. He acted on behalf of the nation and not because he, personally, stood to gain anything. In suppressing the coup, the king was representing his people.[8]

"There is no reason to believe that constitutional monarchy will be less viable in the twenty-first century than in the twentieth, when it proved to be the most reliable framework of liberal democratic states."[9]

—*Eric Hobsbawn,
British historian*

A similar event is part of Thailand's history. There, a military coup led to the installation of the coup's leader, an army commander, as prime minister in 1992. Pro-democracy protesters demonstrated and soldiers fired on them. In response, King Bhumibol called the prime minister and the leader of the pro-democracy movement to his palace. During a televised audience in which viewers saw the political leaders kneeling before him in accordance with cultural protocol, Bhumibol told the two men to solve the problem peacefully. The result was that the prime minister resigned.

Elections were held, and a civilian government took office.

Finally, a politically neutral monarch has untold value as an adviser to political leaders. He or she can provide advice as well as a historical perspective to the elected officials. The queen and her representatives in the Commonwealth realms, called governors or governors-general, have the right to be consulted, the right to encourage, and the right to warn, according to custom and convention. In the United Kingdom, this power is put into practice in weekly confidential meetings between the British prime minister and the queen.

Popularity of the Monarchy

Monarchies have advantages and disadvantages, but polls show that a majority of people are in favor of them.

- Among the Scandinavian monarchies, a 2010 poll showed 56 percent of Swedes want to retain their monarchy, although that is a drop from 68 percent in 2003.[10] In Norway, support for the monarchy was about 75 percent in 2004.[11] Denmark posts the highest amount of support for its monarchy, at about 82 percent.[12]

- A 2009 poll conducted by the British Broadcasting Corporation found 76 percent of the 1,000 people questioned wanted the monarchy to continue after the Queen.[13]

- A 2008 poll in the Netherlands showed 70 percent of respondents wanted to keep the monarchy, while 25 percent thought the nation should become a republic.[14]

- In Spain, 65 percent of respondents to a 2007 poll favored keeping the monarchy, while almost 23 percent expressed support for a republic.[15]

- In New Zealand, which shares Queen Elizabeth II with 15 other countries, 53 percent of the respondents in a 2010 poll rejected the idea of becoming a republic with a New Zealander as head of state, compared to 32 percent who wanted to become a republic.[16] In a 2009 poll, 45 percent of respondents wanted Prince Charles to become their king after the death of Queen Elizabeth II, while 43 percent said they wanted to become a republic.[17]

- Australia held a referendum in 1999 regarding whether the country should become a presidential republic. Fifty-five percent voted to keep the monarchy.[18]

- In Japan, 82 percent of poll respondents wanted to keep the monarchy, according to a report in *The Times of India*.[19]

The fact that monarchies are favored in many nations implies they have value. Proponents say the value they hold includes the ability to promote stability and unity, to instill national pride in societies with many ethnic backgrounds and to be a neutral zone amid political fractiousness. One more objective for which they all strive, certainly, is longevity. ⌘

Quick Facts

Definition of Monarchy

Monarchy is a system of government in which power is held by one person, usually for life and usually because of heredity. The power can be held absolutely or nominally. An absolute monarch is one who holds and executes all the power. He or she sets national policy, makes laws, and has the sole authority to declare war. A nominal monarch is one who acts only as guardian of the power. Other institutions, such as a parliament, exercise the power by making laws and carrying them out.

Well-Known Monarchies

As of June 2010, 44 countries had monarchies. Among them are the United Kingdom and Japan, which are constitutional monarchies with nominal monarchs, and Saudi Arabia and Vatican City, which are absolute monarchies.

Organization of Monarchies

Most monarchies have an executive branch of government with the monarch serving as head of state and a prime minister serving as head of government; a legislative branch, generally with two chambers and some elected members; and a judiciary with appointed judges.

Main Leadership Positions

Monarchs can include kings, queens, princes, sultans, emirs, or emperors. In parliamentary democracies, the monarch is head of state and performs ceremonial duties. The prime minister is the head of government. In stronger monarchies, the monarch is both head of state and head of government, and legislative bodies are merely advisory.

Ancient Monarchies

Monarchies arose in the ancient world from tribal chiefdoms. They existed in many ancient civilizations, including Sumer (modern-day Iraq), Egypt, and China.

Historic Monarchs

- Alexander the Great, Macedonia (Greece), 336 BCE. Conqueror who expanded kingdom from Greece in Europe to Persia in Asia and Egypt in Africa.

- King John, England, 1199. In 1215, he signed the Magna Carta to end a dispute with English nobility, placing the English monarchy under a written law for the first time.

- Kublai Khan, Mongolia and China, 1260. Created Yuan dynasty in China. Controlled an area that stretched from the Black Sea in Eastern Europe to the Pacific Ocean and from Siberia to Afghanistan.

- Louis XIV, France, 1643. Reigned for 72 years. Ruled absolutely under the theory of divine right of kings.

- Louis XVI, France, 1774. King during the French Revolution, he was beheaded in 1793, followed shortly thereafter by his wife, Marie Antoinette.

- Nicholas II, Russia, 1894. The last emperor of Russia, he abdicated in 1917. Shortly thereafter, the country became a communist state and Nicholas and his family were executed.

- Hirohito, Japan, 1926. Emperor of Japan during World War II. In surrender, he gave up much of the monarchy's power.

How Power Shifts

In most monarchies, the throne changes hands through heredity. Generally it is passed down from the monarch to the monarch's child, usually the firstborn male. In Saudi Arabia, the founding king passed the throne to his eldest son, and it has passed since among the founding king's sons by order of seniority. Sometimes, as in Vatican City, the monarch is chosen by election.

Economic Systems

Most monarchies have fairly free market economic systems that allow private enterprise. Governments regulate and tax. Some countries have more government involvement than others in the economy.

The Roles of Citizens

Citizens cannot choose their monarchs in virtually all cases. In those places that have elected monarchies, a specific group of people votes but not the citizens at large. In Andorra, a dual principality, one prince is the elected president of France, and the other is an appointed Roman Catholic bishop. In most constitutional monarchies with parliamentary democracies, citizens vote for the officials who actually govern—the members of their parliament. In strong monarchies, citizens may be able to vote for officials who sit in their legislature, but not all, and those legislative bodies act as consulting bodies rather than lawmaking bodies.

Personal Freedoms and Rights

In democratic constitutional monarchies, citizens vote for their lawmakers and can speak and assemble freely. Criticism and unpopular ideas can appear in the press without government restriction. Opposition to the government can organize. In strong monarchies, the government restricts speech, assembly, press, and religious freedoms.

Organized opposition to the government is restricted or prohibited.

Strengths of Monarchies

- Stability: Monarchs are a constant in an otherwise constantly changing political landscape.

- Unity: Monarchs provide a common national focus for citizens of different backgrounds.

- Neutrality: Monarchs are not politicians subject to election and, therefore, are not beholden to special interests. Neutrality also allows monarchs to mediate disputes between political factions.

- Popularity: Many citizens who live in constitutional monarchies seem to like them.

Weaknesses of Monarchies

- Expensive: Monarchies can cost their citizens a lot of money to maintain.

- Hereditary: Most monarchs get their positions by accident of birth. Their subjects have no say in who rules over them.

- Hierarchical: Monarchy is tied to an outdated social class system, reinforcing class distinctions by giving one family special prominence, government power, wealth, and social standing for no reason other than heredity.

Glossary

abdicate
To formally give up power.

absolute monarchy
A form of government in which supreme power is held by a king or a queen.

anachronism
A person or thing that is chronologically out of place.

ascend
To succeed to or occupy.

bureaucracy
An administrative system characterized by specialized groups, fixed rules, and hierarchy.

cabinet
A government leader's advisers who also head government departments.

constitution
A written document that sets forth the fundamental principles or precedents that govern a state or organization.

constitutional monarchy
A form of government led by a king or queen whose powers are limited by a constitution. It is considered a type of democracy.

democratic
Favoring government by the people.

depose
To remove from a throne or other high position.

despotism
Government rule exercised absolutely and tyrannically.

diplomacy
International negotiations.

dynasty
A succession of rulers from the same family or bloodline.

insurgency
Revolt against a government that is not recognized as an organized revolution.

monarchist
A person who supports and advocates monarchy government in general or a specific monarchy.

pharaoh
The title given to a ruler in ancient Egypt.

primogeniture
A method of succession in which power is passed to the firstborn, or eldest.

principality
The state, office, or authority of a prince.

referendum
Vote of the entire electorate taken on an issue or question.

republic
A form of government in which citizens elect people to represent them.

revolution
Forcible overthrow of a government or social order in favor of a new system.

shoguns
Hereditary military commanders in Japan who ruled the country while the emperors ruled nominally.

succession
The order in which or the rules by which one person follows another to take the throne.

Additional Resources

Selected Bibliography

Cordesman, Anthony H. *Saudi Arabia Enters the Twenty-first Century*. Westport, CT: Praeger, 2003. Print.

Grant, Neil. *Kings & Queens*. London: Collins, 2003. Print.

Hibbert, Christopher. *The Days of The French Revolution*. New York: Morrow Quill, 1981. Print.

Lacey, Robert. *Monarch: The Life and Reign of Elizabeth II*. New York: The Free Press, 2002. Print.

Rude, George. *The French Revolution*. New York: Grove, 1988. Print.

Further Readings

Cavendish, Richard. *Kings and Queens: The Concise Guide*. Newton Abbot, UK: David and Charles, 2007. Print.

Eagles, Robin. *The Rough Guide Chronicle: England*. London: Penguin Books, 2002. Print.

Kummer, Patricia K. *Jordan*. New York: Children's Press, 2007. Print.

Web Links

To learn more about monarchies, visit ABDO Publishing Company online at **www.abdopublishing.com**. Web sites about monarchies are featured on our Book Links page. These links are routinely monitored and updated to provide the most current information available.

Places to Visit

Buckingham Palace
Buckingham Palace Road, London, England
44 020 7766 7300
http://www.royalcollection.org.uk
The official residence of the British monarch since 1837, Buckingham Palace also houses the staff and advisers to the royal family.

The Imperial Palace
Tokyo, Japan
03-3213-1111
http://www.kunaicho.go.jp/e-event/
On January 2, for the New Year's greeting, and December 23, for the emperor's birthday, visitors can enter the inner palace grounds, where the imperial family makes public appearances on a balcony. Guided tours of the palace are offered most days throughout the year with advance reservations.

Palace at Versailles
Versailles, France
33 01 30 83 78 00
http://chateauversailles.fr/prepare-my-visit-/single/tickets-and-rates
Visitors can see the grounds, Trianon Palaces, Marie-Antoinette's Estate, and other exhibitions.

Source Notes

Chapter 1. Queen Elizabeth II, a Modern Monarch

1. Robert Lacey. *Monarch: The Life and Reign of Elizabeth II.* New York: The Free Press, 2002. Print. 66.

2. Ibid. 117.

3. Princess Elizabeth of the United Kingdom. "Twenty-first Birthday Speech." *The Official Website of The British Monarchy.* n.d. Web. 10 June 2010.

4. Jeffrey Stinson. "On Queen's 80th, Britons Ask: Is Monarchy Licked?" *USA Today.* 3 May 2006. Web. 10 June 2010.

5. "Modern Monarchy." *Monarchy.org.nz.* n.d. Web. 1 Oct. 2010.

6. "Happy and Glorious." *Ottawa Citizen.* 7 June 2010. Web. 11 June 2010.

7. Jeffrey Stinson. "On Queen's 80th, Britons Ask: Is Monarchy Licked?" *USA Today.* 3 May 2006. Web. 10 June 2010.

8. "Happy and Glorious." *Ottawa Citizen.* 7 June 2010. Web. 11 June 2010.

Chapter 2. What Is a Monarchy?

1. "God Save the Queen." *Lyrics Mode.* n.d. Web. 1 Oct. 2010.

2. Woodrow Wilson. "Constitutional Government in the United States I." *TeachingAmericanHistory.org.* n.d. Web. 21 June 2010.

3. "The Monarchy in Sweden." *Swedish Royal Court.* n.d. Web. 18 June 2010.

4. "Fundamental Law of Vatican City State." *Vatican City State.* 26 November 2000. Web. 20 June 2010.

5. *The Phrase Finder.* n.d. Web. 4 Nov. 2010.

6. "2009 Human Rights Report: Saudi Arabia." *U.S. Department of State.* 11 March 2010. Web. 21 June 2010.

7. "Basic Law of Government." *The Middle East Information Network.* n.d. Web. 21 June 2010.

8. "Human Rights in Kingdom of Saudi Arabia: Report 2009." *Amnesty International.* n.d. Web. 21 June 2010.

Chapter 3. Key Monarchies in World History

1. Richard Hooker. "Rome: Julius Caesar." *Washington State University.* 1996. Web. 24 June 2010.

2. Voltaire. *General Essay on the History and Manners and Spirit of Nations.* 1756. Web. 25 June 2010.

Chapter 4. The Origins and Expansion of Power

1. *Thinkexist.com*. n.d. Web. 1 Oct. 2010.
2. Ebenezer Cobham Brewer. *Dictionary of Phrase and Fable*. Philadelphia: Henry Altemus Company, 1898. Web. 1 Oct. 2010.

Chapter 5. Staying in Power

1. Randeep Ramesh. "Bhutan crowns new king." *Guardian. co.uk*. 6 Nov. 2008. Web. 5 July 2010.
2. "National Day Address." *Keys to Bhutan*. 17 December 2005. Web. 5 July 2010.
3. Matthew Rosenberg. "King of Bhutan Gives Up His Absolute Monarchy." *The Independent*. 24 March 2008. Web. 5 July 2010.
4. Miranda Carter. "How to Keep Your Crown." *History Today*. Oct. 2009. Print. 5–6.
5. Robert Lacey. *Monarch: The Life and Reign of Elizabeth II*. New York: The Free Press, 2002. Print. 57.
6. "The Emperor." *GlobalSecurity.org*. n.d. Web. 19 July 2010.
7. David McNeill. "What Role Japan's Imperial Family?" *Znet*. 18 December 2005. Web. 9 July 2010.
8. Aisha Labi. "Europe's Monarchies: Their Modern Majesties." *TIME*. 3 June 2000. Web. 5 July 2010.
9. Anthony Cordesman. *Saudi Arabia Enters the Twenty-first Century*. Westport, CT: Praeger. 2003. Print. 133.
10. "Human Rights in the Hashemite Kingdom of Jordan." *Amnesty International*. 2009. Web. 1 Oct. 2010.

Chapter 6. Succession in Monarchies

1. Emi Doi. "Japanese Citizens Celebrate Arrival of Little Prince." *The Seattle Times*. 7 Sept. 2006. Web. 30 June 2010.
2. Andrew Pierce. "U-turn on Royal Succession Law Change." *The Daily Telegraph*. 28 April 2008. Web. 30 June 2010.
3. Emi Doi. "Japanese Celebrate Birth of Royal Heir." *McClatchy Newspapers*. 6 Sept. 2006. Web. 8 June 2010.
4. Simon Henderson. "New Saudi Rules on Succession: Will They Fix the Problem?" *The Washington Institute for Near East Policy*. 25 Oct. 2006. Web. 20 June 2010.

Chapter 7. How Monarchies End

1. "Nepal Votes to Abolish Monarchy." *BBC News*. 28 May 2008. Web. 1 July 2010.

2. Binaj Gurubacharya. "Nepal's King Dismisses Government." *USA Today*. 1 Feb. 2005. Web. 1 July 2010.

3. Ashis Chakrabarti. "Witnessing the Decline and Fall of a Monarchy." *China Daily*. 5 June 2008. 9. Web. 11 June 2010.

4. George Rude. *The French Revolution*. New York: Grove, 1988. Print. 54.

5. Christopher Hibbert. *The Day of the French Revolution*. New York: Morrow Quill, 1980. Print. 188.

6. Ibid. 189.

7. Richard Hooker. "Selim II." *The Ottomans*. Washington State. 1999. Web. 3 July 2010.

Chapter 8. Living in a Monarchy

1. David E. Kaplan. "Of Bedouins and Bombings." *U.S. News & World Report*. 24 Nov. 2003. Print. 28.

2. Sonia Verma. "Religious Police in Saudi Arabia Arrest Mother for Sitting with a Man." *The Times*. 7 Feb. 2008. Web. 15 July 2001.

Chapter 9. Monarchies and International Relations

1. "Obama, Saudi King Pray for the Media." *USA Today*. 29 June 2010. Web. 17 July 2010.

2. Ibid.

3. Ibid.

4. Saba—Yemen News Agency. "GCC to Set Up Regional Human Rights Watchdog: Report." *Yemen News Agency*. 16 July 2010. Web. 17 July 2010.

5. Nawab Khan. "EU, GCC Determined to Expand Economic Cooperation." *Kuwait News Agency.* 12 July 2010. Web. 17 July 2010.

6. Department of Public Information. "Security Council Imposes Additional Sanctions on Iran, Voting 12 in Favour to 2 Against, with 1 Abstention." *United Nations Security Council*. 9 June 2010. Web. 17 July 2010.

7. "The World Factbook." *Central Intelligence Agency*. n.d. Web. 1 Oct. 2010.

8. Ibid.

9. Ibid.

10. Lee P. Ruddin. "The Enduring Usefulness of the British Monarchy." *History News Network*. 10 Oct. 2010. Web.

Chapter 10. Monarchies, Media, and Celebrity

1. Robert Lacey. *Monarch: The Life and Reign of Elizabeth II*. New York: The Free Press, 2003. Print. 275.

2. Roy Greensdale. "Fear of Backlash Muzzles the Media." *Guardian.co.uk*. 8 Dec. 2000. Web. 10 July 2010.

3. Robert Lacey. *Monarch: The Life and Reign of Elizabeth II.* New York: The Free Press, 2003. Print. 227.

4. Roy Greensdale. "Fear of Backlash Muzzles the Media." *Guardian.co.uk.* 8 Dec. 2000. Web. 10 July 2010.

5. Johann Hari. "Will He, Won't He?" *New Statesman.* 7 January 2002. Web. 11 July 2010.

6. "Swiss Man Faces Jail for *Lèse Majesté.*" *Telegraph.co.uk.* 13 Mar. 2007. Web. 6 July 2010.

Chapter 11. Downsides to Modern Monarchies

1. Mohamed El Dahshan. "Money Talks at Royal Weddings." *The Guardian.* 19 June 2010. Web. 1 Oct. 2010.

2. Ibid.

3. Tatiana Serafin. "The World's Richest Royals." *Forbes.com.* 7 July 2010. Web. 4 Oct. 2010.

4. Grice, Elizabeth. "The Queen: What Price a Global Superstar?" *Telegraph.co.uk.* 7 July 2010. Web. 1 Oct. 2010.

5. Richard Palmer. "Our Royal Family Is Most Expensive in Europe." *Express.co.uk.* 3 July 2010. Web. 1 July 2010.

6. Ibid.

7. Ibid.

8. Annual Report: The Royal House of Denmark 2009. Web. 1 Oct. 2010.

9. Gale Eisenstodt. "Behind the Chrysanthemum Curtain." *Atlantic Online.* November 1998. Web. 1 Oct. 2010.

10. David McNeill. "What Role Japan's Imperial Family?" *Znet.* 18 Dec. 2005. Web. 9 July 2010.

11. "Mswati III, King of Swaziland." *The New York Times.* 5 Sept. 2008. Web. 1 Oct. 2010.

12. William Lee Adams. "Royal in Recession: Prince Charles Embraces Frugality." *Time.* 3 July 2010. Web. 9 July 2010.

13. Lewis Holden. "The Monarchy Enhances the Power of Politicians." *Independent Australia.* 7 July 2010. Web. 8 July 2010.

14. Robert Verkaik. "Charles Draws Fire for Over-Use of Royal Pen." *Nzherald.co.nz.* 2 July 2010. Web. 9 July 2010.

15. "Does the Monarchy Still Matter?" *New Statesman.* 9 July 2009. Web. 28 June 2010.

16. David McNeill. "What Role Japan's Imperial Family?" *Znet.* 18 Dec. 2005. Web. 9 July 2010.

17. Thomas Paine. "Common Sense." 1776. *USHistory.org.* Web. 4 Nov. 2010.

18. Claire Rayner. "Is This Their Last Hurrah? Let's Hope So…" *Guardian.co.uk.* 6 Aug. 2000. Web. 8 July 2010.

19. "Does the Monarchy Still Matter?" *New Statesman.* 9 July 2009. Web. 28 June 2010.

Chapter 12. Positive Attributes of Modern Monarchies

1. "What Is Constitutional Monarchy?" *The Official Website of the British Monarchy*. n.d. Web. 6 July 2010.

2. "Does the Monarchy Still Matter?" *New Statesman*. 9 July 2009. Web. 19 July 2010.

3. Aisha Labi. "Europe's Monarchies: Their Modern Majesties." *Time*. 3 July 2002. Web. 5 July 2010.

4. Ibid

5. "Most Dutch Content with Monarchy." *Angus Reid Global Monitor*. 14 May 2008. Web. 7 July 2010.

6. Jeffrey Stinson. "On Queen's 80th, Britons Ask: Is Monarchy Licked?" *USA Today*. 3 May 2006. Web. 10 June 2010.

7. "Hereditary?" *Monarchy New Zealand*. Web. 7 June 2010.

8. "Unifying Presence." *Canada and the World Backgrounder*. May 1999. Print. p. 12–17.

9. "Does the Monarchy Still Matter?" *New Statesman*. 9 July 2009. Web. 19 July 2010.

10. "Royal Wedding Triggers Monarchy Debate in Sweden." *SINA English*. 13 June 2010. Web. 1 Oct. 2010.

11. "Her Royal Highness Ingrid Alexandra." *Norway: the official site in the UK*. 3 Sept. 2009. Web. 1 Oct. 2010.

12. Trond Noren Isaksen. "Strong Support for Danish Monarchy, But Many Want Reforms." *Trondni.blogspot.com*. 12 Apr. 2010. Web. 1 Oct. 2010.

13. "PM and Palace 'Discussed Reform.'" *British Broadcasting Corporation*. 27 Mar. 2009. Web. 1 Oct. 2010.

14. "Most Dutch Content With Monarchy." *Angus Reid Global Monitor*. 14 May 2008. Web. 1 Oct. 2010.

15. "Spaniards Clearly Support the Monarchy." *Angus Reid Global Monitor*. 19 Oct. 2007. Web. 1 Oct. 2010.

16. "New Zealanders Dismiss Becoming a Republic." *Angus Reid Global Monitor*. 22 Mar. 2010.

17. "New Zealand Split on Monarchy's Future." *Angus Reid Global Monitor*. 28 Apr. 2009.

18. "1999 Referendum Report and Statistics." *Australia Electoral Commission*. 9 Aug. 2007. Web. 1 Oct. 2010.

19. Joshua Kurlantzick. "Saved by the Crown." *The Times of India*. 29 May 2010. Web. 4 Nov. 2010.

Index